READY OR NOT — HE IS COMING

Contents

Dedicated to Yeshua's Bride
May you be ready at His coming....

Acknowledgements

First of all, I would like to thank You Jesus, for Your faithfulness to me as part of Your consecrated Bride, over the years – even when I have messed up, been distracted or led astray for a season. Your love and faithfulness endure forever! Thank You Lord for entrusting the words of this book to me… My tongue shall indeed be the pen of a ready writer (Psalm 45:1).

To my hubby Mark, thank you so much for your encouragement and patience as I spent large parts of our evenings working on *Ready or Not…* Your love and support have been immense! You were there in the background, with your prayers, and now that the book is finished, your sense of pride in what I have accomplished is a beautiful witness of what God is doing in our own marriage, I love you darling!

To my parents, thank you for the solid foundation you laid in my life. I am so honoured to have the heritage I have from you both, as a Christian and as a Jewish believer – I have a "double portion"! A lot of what you accomplished, or started to do, became the starting point of my own life, with so much encouragement to "Go for it!" I truly am blessed to call you mum and dad!

To my friends and colleagues at CMJ UK, listening to you as I researched this subject was a huge blessing… Even though you may not have realised I was listening! I also add to that my thanks to Church friends I have had conversations with whilst at City Gates, Ilford, and J28 Church in Derby. Every conversation which sparked a thought or revelation in my heart and mind, every opportunity to teach verbally or write a study has been used to hone and develop the gift of *Ready or Not…* Many of you were privy to my thoughts as I wrote this book, and your support and encouragement was gratefully received, at every stage!

Thank you to the team of people who helped with the preparation of the book for publishing: Jacki Turney and Julie Wilson, thank you for reading through the manuscript checking for errors. Jacki, I know you probably read it more than I did! To my dad (my personal Biblical Hebrew teacher); and to Alex Jacob of CMJ – thank you for checking *Ready or Not…* on a theological level. Your insights and suggestions were gratefully appreciated.

Finally, thank you to Peter Sammons, and all at Glory to Glory for taking a risk with this new author. Your excitement about my book is such an encouragement to me.

Note on translations

There are many translations of the Bible easily available today, especially as the modern language develops and we are able to apply the correct translation of the original Hebrew and Greek texts. I love to vary my study, in using a variety of translations, allowing me to build up a clear picture of what God is saying in His Word, whilst maintaining the integrity of the Scriptures. In this, I have applied the same principles as with my own personal study, and often quote from a modern translation / paraphrase, in order for the text to flow.

However, my favourite translation is the NKJ, so Bible verses are predominantly quoted from the NKJ Bible, unless otherwise stated.

As I am looking at the Jewish Wedding traditions in light of Christian revelation, it seems somewhat fitting to use Jesus and Yeshua interchangeably… Yeshua is His name in Hebrew, with Jesus being the English translation we most commonly recognise. And as I am a Christian of Jewish descent, I wanted to remain true to my heritage by bringing together both the Names in one study, in the hope that I won't alienate Christian or Messianic readers who choose to pick up *Ready or Not*....

Foreword

I warmly endorse the book *Ready or Not...He is Coming* by Stephanie Cottam. This book is a fresh and perceptive exploration of the promises around the Lord's victorious return. The context for this exploration is found within the rich and beautiful Jewish wedding traditions.

Stephanie writes in a lively, reflective and informative style drawing from her own wedding experience and weaving this in with numerous important biblical texts and warm personal insight. I am sure many readers will find within this book much which will delight, encourage and challenge.

I encourage you to buy it, read it and learn from it.

The Revd. Alex Jacob MA, M.Phil
Church's Ministry among Jewish People (CMJ)

Introduction

One night, in January 2011, I was lying in bed thinking and reflecting on the things of the Lord, having listened to a sermon podcast by Greg Laurie of Harvest Christian Fellowship, California. He was speaking on the final battle at Armageddon and the rapture of the Church beforehand. As I reflected on what Greg Laurie had been saying, I heard the Lord as He began to speak very clearly, this message you are about to read. In a whisper, I heard the Lord saying, "Ready or not... Here I come..."

This is not a message for my ears only. There is no "Top Secret" stamped across the top of the cover. There is no whispering in hushed tones, in long, dark corridors. There is no "this message will self-destruct in..." No, this is a message you need to hear! This is a message which is to be proclaimed from house to house, neighbour to neighbour. This is a message which has been spoken throughout history, and is now, with more urgency, being proclaimed louder and louder. Be still, be silent — the Lord speaks. Do you hear Him? The Lord is aroused from His holy habitation. The Lord is ready to move in these days.

Zechariah 2:13 (The Message): *"Quiet, everyone! Shh! Silence before God. Something's afoot in his holy house. He's on the move!"*

James 5:9 (AMP): *"Look! The Judge is [already] standing at the very door."*

There are many references in Scripture to weddings, brides and grooms. So the wedding traditions surrounding Jewish culture during Biblical times are the basis of the message contained within this book. The Wedding is being arranged, the tables are being laid in preparation for the Great Feast, and the Groom is almost ready to collect His Bride.

What does this mean for us in the 21st century? What can we understand of what Jesus taught about marriage in relationship to the Church? How do the principles of Jewish marriage traditions reflect on the second coming of Jesus?

In this book, I hope to glean something from the messages of our Lord, our roots in Jewish traditions, and lay them at your heart's door, hoping that you will open up and let them in to take root in your spirit. The message is loud, the message is strong. The trumpet players are in rehearsals, throats are being cleared, in preparation for the shout. What you do with this is entirely your call, but do something you must! This is not a message which can be ignored, because time is running short.

This is not just a book for the ladies, even though there are many references to "the bride", and even though I generally refer to "she" as opposed to "he" when talking about aspects of preparation. It is understood by the author that men will read this book too.

As the Church, we are all the Bride of Christ, purchased by the blood of Jesus Himself.

Revelation 5:9 (AMP): *"And [now] they sing a new song, saying, You are worthy to take the scroll and to break the seals that are on it, for You were slain (sacrificed), and with Your blood You purchased men* *unto God from every tribe and language and people and nation.*"

We are joined with Him, made one in Him, without division.

Galatians 3:28 (AMP): *"There is [now no distinction] neither Jew nor Greek, there is neither slave nor free,* ***there is not male and female; for you are all one in Christ Jesus***." (Emphasis is author's own.)

So if you are a man reading this, I would ask that you take on board the concept behind the various references to weddings, 'Bride', etc. — for there are lessons which are as important to you as they are to any woman reading this. There is a message contained within this book for you, if you are a believer. And ladies, don't get too caught up in the loveliness of the wonderful preparations of the wedding, as this message is a warning that we should all recognise and take seriously.

Because at the end of the day, when the fullness of time has come, when Jesus returns, He won't ask which gender you are, He will merely draw you unto Himself, as His Bride!

Part of the challenge of this book is that, like a mirror, the Word of God reflects the state of our inner-beings. It causes us to examine ourselves, to search our hearts in the Light of the Word. At one time or another, I – and I'm guessing you too – have become embroiled in the things of the world. I had tried to hide from the Light, as Adam and Eve did in the Garden of Eden, knowing that I was not worthy to stand before Him, naked and ashamed. But, as Adam and Eve found, and as King David acknowledged, there is nowhere to hide from God (Psalm 139:7-12).

When Jesus returns for His Bride, some of us will be ready, some of us will not be ready. I think of the children's game of "Hide and Seek", which draws to an end when all participants have been found. But there are many differences in the very serious matter of the Lord's return, for the old must make way for the new and God's plan will be realised. Wheat and tares will be separated. Those prophecies which are yet to be fulfilled will be fulfilled. There will be divine judgement. God is not slack concerning His promises to us! He longs for us to know Him, as He dwells amongst us (Revelation 21:3), where we will "see His face" (Revelation 22:4)! Where the glory of the Lord "will be our light" (Revelation 21:23), and there will be "no tears, no more death, no sorrow, no more pain" (Revelation 21:4). What a glorious time awaits us, to know our King, as a wife comes to know her husband.

Ready or not . . . He is coming

Chapter One

The Wedding Invitation

I love weddings! I love the excitement from the moment we receive the wedding invitation. I can honestly say I have never received the same wedding invitation twice – each invitation is uniquely designed or chosen by the bride and groom, and usually gives us an indication of what we can expect from the day: the theme we can expect to see or the colours we should avoid, if we don't want to clash with the bridesmaids. I love it! From that moment on, the excitement for the guests begins to build. We start to wonder: Oh my days, what am I going to wear? I need to go shopping — new outfit, new shoes, new bag, accessories, make-up to match, nails, feet… *boy*! While some people decide they will try to lose weight – particularly if the bride or groom is a close family member or friend. Hey! We all want to look good in those immortal pictures.

I remember the run-up to my own wedding in May 2010. Even though I was the bride, I was fairly relaxed when it came to "the diet". I thought I looked OK at a size 12. I suppose I could have done with shedding a few pounds — you know how it is. But I'll be honest, compared with some of my friends I was so lazy when it came to it! Some of the girls put me to shame with the efforts they were prepared to go to for my big day! And I relished being invited round to view the outfits they were planning to wear – I think they only did this to make sure they had avoided the shame which would have come with wearing the same colour as the bridesmaids. This wasn't a difficult task for anybody who knew me, they could very easily work out they should avoid wearing pink!

The wedding invitation provides us with an indication of what is expected from us as a wedding guest, and believe me, there are many expectations! Firstly, the timing. One of the most frustrating things, as any bride-to-be will tell you, is that of the "non-responder". I mean, seriously, the invitation makes it easy for the guest to reply: email, phone call, text — even with a prepaid stamped addressed card we just have to tick the correct box and post it off. And yet still there are delays in people's responses.... *Why Lord, why?*

Inevitably this leads to the poor bride-to-be having to chase her guests for a reply, on top of all the other preparations she has on her "to do" list. You have been invited. It is your honour as a guest to be invited; it is not the bride or groom's honour to have invited you, and so they shouldn't really have to chase you around asking whether you can be there. The wedding will still go ahead whether you are there or not! The bride and groom are the ones for whom the day is most important.

Which leads me to a very special RSVP....

Matthew 22:1-4: *And Jesus answered and spoke to them again by parables and said: "The kingdom of heaven is like a certain king who arranged a marriage for his son, and sent out his servants to call those who were invited to the wedding; and they were not willing to come. Again, he sent out other servants, saying, 'Tell those who are invited, "See, I have prepared my dinner; my oxen and fatted cattle are killed, and all things are ready. Come to the wedding."'*

This is it, people. This is the wedding invitation.

A lot of invitations are sent on behalf of the parents of the bride and groom, or the parents of the bride, or groom alone. In this case, the invitation has been sent by the Father of the Groom.

The king is a depiction of God Himself. The Creator of the world; the One who made you; the One who knows the end from the beginning, He is the One who has sent an invitation to you. His Son Jesus Christ is the Groom. Oh what a magnificent Groom He will make. Have you heard His love story — His great romance of His beautiful Bride-to-be? Wow! What a story! Don't worry, if you haven't, He's not shy about how much He loves her, nor of the fact that He gave up everything for her!

Let's have a glimpse into the Greatest Romance you will ever encounter....

God's Great Romance

As you read through the Bible, it is very easy to get a sense of the love God has for His people and the sadness He feels at the way He has been treated by us throughout history. We have rejected God time and time again, not just you and I as individuals, but mankind as a whole has rejected Him since the time sin entered the world. But God's desire is still for us to be in a relationship with Him. He desires us, so He made a way for us to be with Him. Jesus is the human representation of God's love, the means by which God demonstrates His love to the world, in a way for us to totally understand – and some of us, over time, have "got it"!

God's desire is for us to know Him, really know Him. To look for Him with our whole hearts so He can reveal

Himself to us. He desires for us to be in a relationship with Him, to pursue Him as none other. He has left us clues of His love throughout His creation, in every nook and cranny, if we will only recognise it:

Song of Songs 2:10-13 (The Message): *"Get up, my dear friend, fair and beautiful lover—come to me! Look around you: Winter is over; the winter rains are over, gone! Spring flowers are in blossom all over. The whole world's a choir—and singing! Spring warblers are filling the forest with sweet arpeggios. Lilacs are exuberantly purple and perfumed, and cherry trees fragrant with blossoms. Oh, get up, dear friend, my fair and beautiful lover—come to me!"*

Oh what a beautiful picture of God's love for us.

The Beginning[1]

Psalm 104:5-31 (NLT): *You placed the world on its foundation so it would never be moved. You clothed the earth with floods of water, water that covered even the mountains. At your command, the water fled; at the sound of your thunder, it hurried away. Mountains rose and valleys sank to the levels you decreed. Then you set a firm boundary for the seas, so they would never again cover the earth. You make springs pour water into the ravines, so streams gush down from the mountains. They provide water for all the animals, and the wild donkeys quench their thirst. The birds nest beside the streams and sing among the branches of the trees. You send rain on the mountains from your heavenly home, and you fill the earth with the fruit of your labour. You cause grass to grow for the livestock and plants for people to use. You allow them to produce food from* *the earth—wine to make them glad, olive oil to soothe their skin, and bread to give them strength. The trees of the Lord are well cared for—the cedars of Lebanon that he planted. There the birds make their nests, and the storks make their homes in the cypresses. High in the mountains live the wild goats, and the rocks form a refuge for the hyraxes. You made the moon to mark the seasons, and the sun knows when to set. You send the darkness, and it becomes night, when all the forest animals prowl about. Then the young lions roar for their prey, stalking the food provided by God. At dawn they slink back into their dens to rest. Then people go off to their work, where they labour until evening. O Lord, what a variety of things you have made! In wisdom you have made them all. The earth is full of your creatures. Here is the ocean, vast and wide, teeming with life of every kind, both large and small… May the glory of the Lord continue forever! The Lord takes pleasure in all he has made!*

Most of us will have an understanding of the Creation of the world – regardless of our beliefs – from our reading of the first book of the Bible: *Beresheit* – "In the Beginning" – Genesis. What I love about knowing God as the Creator of the heavens and the earth is the revelation of His invisible nature and attributes in every aspect of His creation (Romans 1:20). He took the void, dark, formless-ness, and from it created the heavens and the earth. Nothing appeared by accident… none of us are just here by chance… no! Every part was carefully designed and planned. Even you! You were skilfully and purposefully knit together in your mother's womb (See Psalm 139).

I often enjoy just standing still and consider the wondrous works of God (Just as Job and his friends did, see Job 37:14, and as have many countless men and women before me!). As we consider God's Great Romance, I challenge you to also "stand still and consider the wondrous works of God". For it is when we do that we can look, in stunned awe, at how He placed the world on its foundation – so that it can never be moved (Psalm 104:5). Oh how the depth of the detail surrounding creation that we find throughout Scripture, is an amazing testimony to how accurate the Word of God… for all Scripture is God-breathed.

As we pause for a moment, in the business of our daily life, we can clearly see God's love and faithfulness in His creation and realise how precious we are to Him when we realise He holds all things together (Colossians 1:17). David often acknowledged God's sustenance of life as he wrote his Psalms, for example in Psalm 104 he writes, "*… You open your hand to feed them, and they are richly satisfied. But if you turn away from them, they panic. When you take away their breath, they die and turn again to dust. When you give them your breath, life is created, and you renew the face of the earth.*" (Psalm 104:28-30)

But why does God do this? Is it to reveal Himself to us – the people He loves? Is it to demonstrate His glory and splendour to His creation, so we would be drawn to Him and worship Him? Is it because He loves us and takes pleasure in us? The answer to this is a resounding "YES!" to all of the above!

As we examine the Beginning, we catch a glimpse of how things "should be" and how they will once again be, when the old gives way to the new… As we look at the Beginning, we see how God walked among us. Among our ancestors, Adam and Eve. What a delightful scene we can envisage, as God walked with His creation in a Garden created to be perfection, where every beautiful element was a reflection of God's beauty and majesty (Job 40:10, Romans 1:20), and where even now the heavens declare the resplendent glory of God! (Psalm 19:1-6) He made mankind in His image, we are a reflection of His image, made according to His likeness (Genesis 1:26). He delights in YOU, dear reader! Take a look at yourself in the mirror, and try to really comprehend what this means, for Elohim (the plural form of God's Hebrew name which is the first Name used in the Scriptures) to have made you in His image! Glance at the rainbow in the sky, and be reminded of God's covenant with mankind (Genesis 9:16), even after we sinned and rejected Him. Glance at the night sky and see the stars showing off His handiwork (Psalm 19:2), in an impressive display of His glory and majesty. Stand silent next to the babbling brook and think on the sound from that first day, as the morning stars sang together and all the sons of God shouted for joy, when the foundations of the world were laid (Job 38:7). Let His majesty take your breath away!

Psalm 8:3-5: *When I consider Your heavens, the work of Your fingers, The moon and the stars, which You have ordained, What is man that You are mindful of him, and the son of man that You visit him? For You have made him a little lower than the angels, And You have crowned him with glory and honour.*

And yet, who are we that God would even consider us, think on us, or even delight in us anyway? From the very beginning, before even the foundations of the world had been laid, God created the world with us in mind, choosing us to be with Him, adopted into His family.

Ephesians 1:4: *... just as He chose us in Him before the foundation of the world....*

As He spoke each thing into being – the light, the darkness; the morning, the evening; the waters and the land; the plants, the fruit, the seeds; the sun, the moon and the stars for the seasons; days and years; the abundance of living creatures in the water, in the sky and upon the earth – God knew exactly what He was doing, for He knew the end from the beginning (Isaiah 46:10). He knew what we would need, and made sure that we would be catered for with food to eat and plants, fruit and herbs to use (Genesis 1:11), according to what we could use (Psalm 104:14). That God would have been mindful of us, even from the beginning demonstrates His Great Romance to us. That God would even consider being in a relationship with us, let alone that He originally placed us in the most beautiful of His created places – in the Garden where He walked.

In the beginning, we can see how God repeatedly declared His creation (as He originally made it) to be good: "God saw that it was good" as He looked over all He had made. Consider for a moment what this means. First of all, everything originally had a purpose in God's plan. We think 'good' means something that feels nice for us, serving our own comfort and convenience. But when used of God, the Bible shows us throughout that it signals absolute righteousness. The first moments between God and His creation were perfectly righteous! That is why it was so utterly devastating when humanity succumbed to temptation, disobeyed and rebelled against God. Throwing aside the perfect relationship we had with Him for the sake of "all that is in the world— the lust of the flesh, the lust of the eyes, and the pride of life." (1 John 2:16)

As we breathe in the scene before us, we realise how even the earth groans, as it waits in anticipation for things to be restored, once again, to God's original plan: ***Romans 8:22:*** *For we know that the whole creation groans and labours with birth pangs together until now.* In the beginning, the created order was made perfect and good in the true, biblical sense: righteous, holy, obedient to the Maker. And ultimately, on that Great Day, all will once again be as He originally intended: righteous, holy, perfect, inhabited only by people who are righteous, holy, and perfect.

And yet it is through Yeshua, we see how everything comes from Him and exists by His power and is intended for His glory (Romans 11:36). We cannot be independent of the Bridegroom – for it is through Him we are sustained – He is the Creator and unrelenting giver of life itself. As we unpack the theme of this book, we must constantly bear in mind this eternal purpose of God, as declared in Genesis.

The Middle

Within each one of us, God places the desire for us to know Him, to be in a relationship with Him. But most of us, since the beginning of time, since the fall of the first Adam and Eve, have attempted to fill the place in our hearts with anything we can see, touch or hold. We tried to make a golden representative of "God" when He brought us out of Egypt, and ever since then, humanity has made statues and given them the title of being a god. We have chased after people and things to fill the void we feel deep within our hearts. We have pursued the things the world tells us are worthy of our attention and affections. We left God behind on the side-lines of our hearts, grieving for His love, grieving for His Bride to look around her at the display of His love for her. But she didn't look up.

She didn't acknowledge Him.

She didn't notice.

So He sent His Son Jesus to come and walk amongst us, a magnificent display of God's love and grace.

Jesus didn't come to earth blinded to God's expectations of Him. Jesus knew exactly what He was sent to earth to do, He knew exactly why He came to walk amongst mankind.

Philippians 2:7-8 (NLT): *"Instead, He gave up His divine privileges; He took the humble position of a slave and was born as a human being. When He appeared in human form, He humbled Himself in obedience to God and died a criminal's death on a cross."*

The love Jesus has for His people, led Him to die for us. He is a Friend who loves at all times, who would do anything for us, including laying down His life for us.

John 15: 9-14 (NLT): *"I have loved you even as the Father has loved me. Remain in my love. When you obey my commandments, you remain in my love, just as I obey my Father's commandments and remain in his love. I have told you these things so that you will be filled with my joy. Yes, your joy will overflow! This is my commandment: Love each other in the same way I have loved you. There is no greater love than to lay down one's life for one's friends."*

This is the love, which Jesus demonstrated in such a physical, practical, powerful way, so that through His death we may have life, eternal life; to be given a way into love — the love of the Father, the way of love with our Creator, to have our hearts brought back to our *first love*, to come back into the relationship we were created to be in with God.

That's true love! Wonderful love! Perfect love!

But there's more. Jesus didn't die and that's it – end of story. He rose again, and has gone to heaven, where He is making preparations for us to receive His love, to be with Him forever. He is making preparations once again, to create a place of beauty for His Bride, a place which she will delight in, which will allow her to be reflected in all her glory.

John 14:1-3 (NLT): *"Don't let your hearts be troubled. Trust in God, and trust also in me. There is more than enough room in my Father's home. If this were not so, would I have told you that I am going to prepare a place for you? When everything is ready, I will come and get you, so that you will always be with me where I am."*

This is the Great Romance, greater than any *West Side Story* or *Gone With The Wind*; greater than any fairy-tale or chick-flick film! Even though the Groom was rejected time and time again by the Bride, He chased her throughout history, revealing His love for her over and over again, until she recognises Him and accepts Him. And then there will be great rejoicing at the wedding feast – the greatest day which is yet to come – when the Groom will finally receive His Bride to Himself for ever… the *real* King and I!

Wow! What a romance! What love!

Chapter Two

RSVP

An invitation has been issued to each of us to *the* Wedding of all weddings. Any wedding you have ever been to, organised, or been involved in – even your own wedding day – will never compare to The Wedding you have ultimately been invited to, which is destined to be held at the end of time. Have you seen your invitation yet? If not, get yourself a Bible, because your invitation is written in there.

And like any wedding you are invited to, the wedding organiser, the Father of the Groom, is waiting for your response. But there's only so much chasing He can do, you know. The onus is on you to respond to the invitation you have been sent, and whether you will be attending or not, on the biggest day for the whole of creation.

Once the invitation has been sent, the guests cannot ignore it. In itself any wedding invitation demands a response of some type. And there are only two responses you can give, before the RSVP deadline date. *Yes, I will be there*, or *No, I won't be there*. Anything else is a fancy dressing-up of one of these two replies.

But, the time is close at hand. The RSVP date is almost upon us. The day of the wedding feast is almost here. It is time to seriously consider and give your answer to the Sender of the invitation.

Before you give Him yours, or if you think you have already sent back your RSVP card, we need to consider a few things. We need to look at what is expected of us, and whether we can deliver what we promise, as a guest at the wedding.

Invitation Acceptance

Once we have accepted the invitation to attend, our names are added to the guest list. When I was arranging my own wedding to my hubby Mark, how I wish I could have set the acceptances in stone, so no one could change their minds! Alas, this was not the case, and we soon learned where the delete button was, in our computerised list!

We are entitled to change our minds, things come up. I understand that. But there are consequences for the wedding organisers to these changes in our decision. Alterations have to be made to the running of the day.

I went to the wedding of a friend who had people accept her wedding invitation, only then they did not bother turning up on the day. She was so upset. It hadn't been a cheap affair she had organised. Spaces with name-tags remained empty, and food which had been served, remained uneaten. I remember the ushers – and even the groom himself, running around trying to fill the spaces with other guests who had turned up, but hadn't been invited to the Wedding Breakfast, and their faithfulness to the wedding couple was rewarded. People, who had expected to fund their own food for the afternoon, found they were able to enjoy the sumptuous menu prepared on behalf of the bride and groom.

As we can see from the following passage in Matthew, my friend was not alone in this experience. People have behaved this way so often, Jesus was able to use it within

His illustration:
Matthew 22: 4-6: *"'See, I have prepared my dinner; my oxen and fatted cattle are killed, and all things are ready. Come to the wedding.' But they made light of it and went their ways, one to his own farm, another to his business. And the rest seized his servants, treated them spitefully, and killed them."*

But the Father of the Groom was not about to allow the wedding food to go to waste. Just as my friend had done, the invitation was extended to anyone and everyone, so the seats could all be filled.

Matthew 22:10: *"So those servants went out into the highways and gathered together all whom they found, both bad and good. And the wedding hall was filled with guests."*

How frustrating! You'd think people would appreciate the bride and groom's thoughtfulness in inviting them to celebrate their special day.

Or what about the guest who accepts the invitation and then misses the wedding! I have a confession to make – they say it's good for the soul! I was going to another friend's wedding, and could not, for the life of me, decide what to wear. I hadn't had the opportunity to go shopping, so spent the morning standing in front of my wardrobe staring at the rows of clothes in front of me thinking, "I've got nothing to wear!" I eventually settled on a dress I had bought in the January sales, which had not had an airing yet, and decided to wear it to the wedding. I quickly applied some make-up, then realised I had no shoes to go with the dress. Oh my days! Now what? I tried to find some dressy shoes in the deepest darkest recesses of my cupboard and settled on a pair of multi-coloured strappy heels. It looked OK teamed with a small black clutch-bag and pashmina. My poor hubby (to be – at that stage), little did he realise what he was letting himself in for!

So we drove to the Church, using the satnav to guide us to the remote location. We knew we had the right Church when we saw the bridal car a few hundred feet ahead of us. Oh no! We were so late. The bride was on time, but I was late! And I still needed to park the car, then walk, very quickly (in heels!), to the Church. By the time we reached the Church entrance, the bride was out of the car, had already had her pre-wedding pictures taken by the photographer and was in position, ready to go! "Sorry," I whispered as I squeezed past my friend, followed by "you look gorgeous", as we ran into the Church to find a seat.

I hadn't been prepared, in the slightest. But we weren't the only ones — not that it made me feel any better. After the bride had made her entry and was in position next to her groom, more guests tumbled through the door, just as the doors were closed for the ceremony.

Matthew 25:10 reminds us that once the Bride and Heavenly Groom are in position, the doors to the wedding will be shut: "*... the bridegroom came, and those who were ready went in with him to the wedding; and the door was shut.*" This is one wedding when a close call would be too much of a risk to take. Once the doors are shut, they are shut.

At the time Jesus was sharing this, He wouldn't have needed to spell out what this meant. Jewish wedding etiquette stated that no one could enter the wedding celebrations after this point, once the doors had been shut. No matter how close they thought they were to the bridal couple, or their families, the doors would not be opened to them after this point.

Once we accept Jesus as the prophesied Messiah,

once we accept Him into our hearts and lives, and acknowledge Him as our soon returning King, our names are added to the ultimate Guest List — The Lamb's Book of Life!

Revelation 20:12: *And I saw the dead, small and great, standing before God, and books were opened. And another book was opened, which is the Book of Life.*

Once our names are written in, Jesus has promised to help us to overcome the things of the world, in order that our names will remain on the list.

Revelation 3:5: *"He who overcomes shall be clothed in white garments, and I will not blot out his name from the Book of Life".*

This is the most important Guest List you will ever have your name written on, and to not be written in it has an eternal impact:

Revelation 13:8: *All who dwell on the earth will worship him, whose names have not been written in the Book of Life of the Lamb slain....* [author's note: 'him' refers to the beast]

Revelation 20:15: *"And anyone not found written in the Book of Life was cast into the lake of fire."*

In refusing the invitation, we refuse Yeshua Himself. By refusing the Eternity Yeshua offers us, we accept an eternal life with the beast — the enemy of the Groom — the anti-Christ:

Revelation 17:8: *"The beast that you saw was, and is not, and will ascend out of the bottomless pit and go to perdition. And those who dwell on the earth will marvel, whose names are not written in the Book of Life from the foundation of the world, when they see the beast that was, and is not, and yet is."*

Have you really thought about your response to your invitation?

Once You Accept, Get Ready…

Once you have checked your diary, shuffled dates around and sent back your invitation RSVP with your acceptance, it's time to start getting ready.

Two friends of ours were getting married a couple of months after Mark and I had returned from honeymoon. It was great having him in the house before I left for work, he was able to let me know *before* I left home – therefore saving me a shameful moment – if what I was wearing was too revealing or had unexpectedly ripped in an embarrassing place. But the weekend of this wedding, Mark needed to be away, and so I didn't have that extra pair of eyes. Plus, because of space limitations, I'd had to dispose of my full-length mirror — the one I had used prior to Mark's moving in. I'm sure you can almost see where I am going!

I decided to wear a gorgeous long, pink dress I had bought for my honeymoon; it looked great against my tanned skin, and anyway, pink is my favourite colour. Now, ladies, let me tell you this one thing – guys, if your lady is close-by, help her out with this bit – what looks great on the beach or on the deck of a cruise liner doesn't have the same effect when you are in a Church with a ray of light shining through. Obviously, on my honeymoon, I was less worried about how see-through the material was, more so because I was wearing it over swimming gear!

As I entered the Church where the wedding was to take place, I glided elegantly down the centre aisle, walking gracefully toward my friends in the third row from the front of the Church – great position to watch the ceremony. They were frantically waving and I was thinking, "Alright luvies, I'm coming, keep yer arm in yer socket!" I reached the end of the pew where they were, and was rather unceremoniously pulled into the row of seats.

"You're on show," one of the girls whispered to me. How could I possibly be on show? I was wearing a long floaty dress, not a skirt and top which didn't fit properly! She continued: "as you walked down the aisle, the light shone right through your dress, revealing everything. We know what colour knickers you're wearing!"

Oh my days! The shame! Fortunately, I was part of the Worship Team for this wedding, so had arrived early, before any of the guests. The only people who had been a witness to this light-revealing moment were women in the Team I knew I could trust. What could I do though? My modesty was at stake, and there was no way I could stand in front of my friend's wedding guests, revealing everything. I phoned round everyone I could think of who would be coming that afternoon and eventually found someone who had a pair of leggings I could wear underneath the dress. Phew!

Before I'd left the house, I had thought I was ready. I had the dress, I had matching shoes and bag, but I hadn't actually stopped to look in the mirror before I arrived. My shame could have been even worse than it was. I hadn't really prepared for the day, even though I thought I had. I should have tried the outfit on before Mark left for the weekend. I should have realised the material was sheer, and would require something underneath it.

What is on show is not necessarily what people will see. We need to make sure we are ready in every way. I know of people who will get themselves ready for a wedding, or other big event, from the inside out – such as drinking more water than normal, so their skin is clear and looking fresh for the wedding day pictures!

Jesus warns us in ***Luke 12:35 (NLT):*** *"Be dressed ready for service and keep your lamps burning."* Do you see that? "Be dressed ready."

He wasn't referring to the fact that people should be walking around in their top hat and tails all the time, looking as though they are ready to go to a wedding. If we look at the Jewish custom of that day, we will understand, as Jesus' listeners did, exactly what He was saying here, and hopefully, as we go through it, more of Jesus' words will be brought to light.

Chapter Three

Jewish Customs – the Bride Price

The Bible talks a lot about weddings, and how the relationship of the bride to her groom relates to Jesus and those who accept His love and forgiveness. So, if Jesus is called the Groom and God is the Father of the Groom, who is the Bride? As we study together, I hope "who" the Bride is will become clear to you.

Jewish wedding customs at the time of Jesus were very different to our modern day ceremonies. Maybe you have already heard it; maybe you think you know how it would have been. Sure, there are things we can glean from Scripture as we read and study it. But there's always something new the Holy Spirit can shed light on. So, I pray His illuminating light will shine on His truth now, as we study the wedding customs from back then, and how they relate to us now.

****

According to Torah traditions, marriage consists of two-stages, set approximately a year apart. The first is *kiddushin*, a formal betrothal or sanctification of the man to the woman, and the second is *nisu'in*, the finalisation of the nuptials.[2]

So, the first major step in a Jewish marriage was the *Kiddushin* or betrothal.[3]

The betrothal was the first step of the formal marriage

covenant. It was customary for the groom, accompanied by his father, to visit the home of his future bride, in order to negotiate with her father a bride-price. Upon payment, the marriage covenant was considered to be firmly established and legally recognised.

In order for there to be a betrothal, there had to be an acceptance on both sides, to enter into a relationship. A man would be pretty embarrassed if he went home and told his father he had found the woman he wanted to marry, without having spoken to her first. She could easily turn around and reject him in front of his father.

When a man spotted a woman he was interested in, whether at a family or friends' gathering, or an informal occasion, he would already know she was not already betrothed to another – a single woman would have her hair uncovered, a married or engaged woman would be wearing a headscarf. (Just as an aside, this is an interesting link to what Paul had written to the Church in Corinth about a woman's head covering). This allowed potential suitors to identify women who were available. He would then approach her and speak with her, to find out what kind of woman she was, and whether the attraction was deeper than mere physical attraction. At this time, she would also learn about him. She would let him know whether or not she was interested, by the way she interacted with him. He may have made the first move, in approaching her. He may have chosen her among her friends. But it was down to her to accept him or not.

In ***John 15:16*** Jesus says, *"You did not choose Me, but I chose you..."* You have been chosen. We have all received the same invitation to enter into a relationship with Jesus. It's down to you whether you choose to accept Him or not.

By accepting his offer, the woman was essentially agreeing to start the marriage process. The Jewish custom did not allow for casual dating. There was no "Let's just hang out and see what happens." Marriage back then was a serious part of life, as boys and girls were trained to serve God, to honour their parents, and how to be a good husband or wife, when the time came for marriage. Women were treated as someone to be honoured, not casually used. A man was looking seriously to be a husband, to be all he could be to his wife and family. There was no room for a casual attitude towards each other or to relationships as a whole.

Jesus takes on this same attitude with us. He loves the Church. He loves His Bride. He doesn't expect us to be in a casual relationship with Him, or to dip in and out of our relationship with Him. Nor does He expect us to use Him for our own gain, or abuse the love He has for us. Neither does Jesus want us to live promiscuously, dancing with the world in an adulterous relationship. No, as we will see, He has chosen us and wants us to be set apart for Him – as a Jewish woman was set apart for her betrothed husband. Jesus was risking more than just His heart by entering into a relationship with you.

When a man had been accepted by the woman he had chosen, he would go home and tell his father he had found the woman he wanted to marry – this may or may not have been a good thing, as the father may have had more information on the woman and her family. Jewish tradition determined that the family was to be involved in the process of marriage and not just the man and the woman. In some respects this was a good thing, as it could protect either party from entering a potentially bad relationship. There was also the danger the woman's family could try to stop her from being with the man just because they didn't like him – with or without good cause.

What of Yeshua's Bride? Does her "family" try to hinder her relationship with her Groom? The answer to this is a resounding "yes!"

John 8:43-44: *Jesus said to them, " Why do you not understand My speech? Because you are not able to listen to My word. You are of your father the devil, and the desires of your father you want to do."*
Jesus describes satan as the father of all lies, indicating to those He addresses His statement to as being "sons" of his because they share in his desires (i.e. to fulfil the lust of the flesh, such as idolatry, sexual immorality, sorcery, selfish ambitions etc… which are contrary to God, walking according to His Spirit as His child [See for example Galatians 5:16-26]).

Paul understood the relationship we had with satan before we became believers in Yeshua. We were all, at one time, subject to him.

Ephesians 2:1-3: *And you He made alive, who were dead in trespasses and sins, in which you once walked according to the course of this world, according to the prince of the power of the air, the spirit who now works in the sons of disobedience, among whom also we all once conducted ourselves in the lusts of our flesh, fulfilling the desires of the flesh and of the mind, and were by nature children of wrath, just as the others.*

Satan is also described as the "god of this age" (2 Corinthians 4:4) — the god of this age who wants to be idolised and exalted above God. So yes, as the "father" of the Bride (before she is adopted under the Fatherhood of God – Galatians 4:7) satan's ultimate desire is to hold you back from entering into the fullness of your destined future with Jesus. He does not want the Bride to be married to the Groom, so he does everything he can to hinder you from your relationship from the moment you accept Yeshua. But at the end of the day, you have made your choice, and your Groom and His Father are on your side – in God you are victorious to overcome the world in His love (Romans 8:37; 1 John 5:4)!

1 Corinthians 15:57: *"Thanks be to God who gives us the victory"*!

The father and son would then visit the girl, with her father, at home and they would discuss the *Shtar Tena'im*, a Document of Conditions laying out the terms of the marriage, including agreeing a *mohar*, a price for the bride. Now ladies, before you get upset at thinking of the injustice at women being sold like meat in a market, think on this. The bride price showed the value of the woman to the world. The more esteemed a family – the higher the bride price would be. And I know you are worth so much to your Groom that He paid *everything* He had for you. This isn't about "women's lib" – this is about the worth of humanity, to the God who made us.

We are all sinners. We have all wronged God by turning away from Him, and grieving Him with our desire for the things of the world, which lead to sin. And so, the bride price was set as the sacrificial offering of Jesus – the Son of God, Himself. The One through Whom we were made and through Whom we are sustained. He lived among us, a sinless life, in order that He may be the only One Who could stand in our place, paying the ultimate price for all our sin. His life for ours. Giving up His life so we can have eternal life.

The price for the Bride Jesus loved was high. Yeshua gave up His throne in heaven, made Himself as nothing, walking amongst His creation as Man, and was obedient to the laws of humanity… even unto the law of death.

He knowingly lived to die for our sins, once and for all. The Ultimate Sacrifice; the Final sin-offering; the mohar. But because of His love for her – He paid it. Because of His love for you, He paid it. You were bought at a very high price. That's how much you are valued by your betrothed Saviour. That's how much you are worth.

Micah 6:3 (The Message): *"Dear people, how have I done you wrong? Have I burdened you, worn you out? Answer! I delivered you from a bad life in Egypt;* ***I paid a good price to get you*** *out of slavery."* (Emphasis is author's own)

1 Corinthians 6:16 (The Message): *Or didn't you realise that your body is a sacred place, the place of the Holy Spirit? Don't you see that you can't live however you please, squandering what* ***God paid such a high price for****?* (Emphasis is author's own)

Romans 8:31 (The Message): *So, what do you think? With God on our side like this, how can we lose? If God didn't hesitate to put everything on the line for us, embracing our condition and exposing himself to the worst by sending his own Son, is there anything else he wouldn't gladly and freely do for us? ... The One who died for us—who was raised to life for us!—is in the presence of God at this very moment sticking up for us. Do you think anyone is going to be able to drive a wedge between us and Christ's love for us? There is no way!*

From the moment the bride price was paid and accepted, the bride was declared to be consecrated or sanctified, set apart exclusively for her bridegroom.

Mark 9:41: *"Or whoever gives you a cup of water to drink in My name,* ***because you belong to Christ****, assuredly, I say to you, he will by no means lose his reward."* (Emphasis is author's own)

1 Corinthians 6:11: *But you were washed, but you were sanctified, but you were justified in the name of the Lord Jesus and by the Spirit of our God.*

Hebrews 10:10: *By that will we have been sanctified through the offering of the body of Jesus Christ once for all.*

The first requirement has been met. The Bride has accepted the offer of betrothal. The bride price was accepted by the Groom and His Father. In the Garden of Gethsemane, just before Jesus was betrayed and arrested, we hear how He wrestled with the obligation He was about to endure on the cross, for the sake of His Bride. Three times He fell to the ground, earnestly asking God to "take the cup" from Him (Matthew 26:39-44); in chapter 4, we look at the significance of the cup. The demand upon Him was so heavy, so overwhelming, so agonising Jesus' "sweat became like great drops of blood falling down to the ground" (Luke 22:44), and yet He knew the price had been set to satisfy the demand for a blood sacrifice necessary to absolve the sin of the world. Only He was pure enough, only He was totally sinless, only He was sanctified holy, only He was suitable to be the sacrifice demanded to cover the sin of the world. ***Matthew 26:42:*** *"O My Father, if this cup cannot pass away from Me unless I drink it, Your will be done."* The price was paid for Yeshua's Bride. The *Shtar Tena'im* had been drawn up and agreed. She now belonged to Him. She was regarded as His. She is considered to be set apart.

What does this "being set apart" mean? It means that by accepting the man's betrothal, the woman enters into the marriage covenant with him. She accepts she will reject the advances of any other man. It means that she accepts she is his wife, and will wait patiently for him to return for her – not grumbling about him, or pretending she is single and available, not promiscuously engaging with other men. She has signed a contract with him and accepts she will be devoted to him, will live her life in accordance with the terms of the marriage covenant, and will make herself ready for his return to take her home.

When we accept the offer to enter into a relationship with Jesus, we accept we now belong to Him. We are His betrothed. We accept the fact we have chosen to be His and His alone, not chasing after other gods or the things which attract others in the world. We enter into a covenant relationship with Him and accept that we will live our lives in accordance with the terms of the marriage covenant.

When the children of Israel first arrived in the wilderness on their way to the Promised Land from Egypt, they encountered God in a most awesome and magnificent way. At Mount Sinai, God was about to meet with His people, to affirm with them He had chosen them as His special treasure (Exodus 19:5). He had arranged to meet with the people after they had accepted His "proposal" to them.

Exodus 19:8: *Then all the people answered together and said, "All that the Lord has spoken we will do." So Moses brought back the words of the people to the Lord.* This statement was their acceptance of Him as their One True God. Now He was going to reveal Himself to them.

As Moses disappeared into the smoke of the mountain to speak with God, we find that God was giving His people a set of standards by which they were to live, in order to honour Him, and live as set apart from other people around them. These formed part of the covenant made between God and His people (us). They were given in order for His people to experience an abundant life.

These are the same standards by which we, as believers, choose to live as part of our covenant with Jesus – not just because the Ten Commandments are a list of "Thou shalt not..." rules, but because we know the importance of living a lifestyle which is different to the way the world lives. We *are not like* [the world], *for you are a chosen people. You are royal priests, a holy nation, God's very own possession* (1 Peter 2:9). We do not live according to the ways of the world, because we are citizens of heaven (Philippians 3:20), and we are waiting for Yeshua to take us home to the place He has prepared for us (John 14:2-3). In the meantime, there is an expectation upon us to live the abundant life God chose for us to live, as we obey His voice and keep His covenant.

When Yeshua taught about the Ten Commandments, He didn't say we don't need to keep them anymore. He said everything we do matters in relation to living by them. Not just our physical actions, but our heart's intentions. Jesus takes us beyond the mere words of the commandments, right to the very centre of what it means to live by them from our hearts. When Jesus gave the "Sermon on the Mount" (Matthew 5-7), He expounded on what it means to "commit adultery" by explaining that adultery is not just the physical act of getting into bed with a married man or woman, it starts with the look of lust (Matthew 5:27-28). Not that we should go around plucking out our eyes or cutting off our hands (see ref. Matthew 5:29-30), but that we should understand the importance of living a lifestyle consecrated to a holy God. So we can show our love for Him by the way we live, and as we are doing this others can see we are in a relationship with Him, and are different to those who are in a relationship with the things of the world. Thus we can freely approach Him with Whom we are in a relationship.

Chapter Four

Jewish Wedding Customs – The Betrothal Cup of Blessing

A betrothal blessing was pronounced over the couple, as they shared a cup of wine together; thus symbolising the covenant relationship had been established between them.

The "Betrothal Blessing" is a two-fold blessing, one over the cup of wine, and the other over the betrothed couple.[4] According to Jewish tradition, it reads something like this:

"Blessed are You Adonai our G-d, King of the universe, Who creates the fruit of the vine.

Blessed are You Adonai our G-d, King of the universe, Who has made us holy through His Commandments, and commanded us regarding illicit relations, and has forbidden to us the betrothed, and has permitted to us those whom we have married through Chuppah and Kiddushin; Blessed are You Adonai, Who makes His nation holy through Chuppah and Kiddushin."

From the actual words contained within the blessing, we can see how the Jewish People acknowledged God as being the One who makes us holy, and of how the couple are consecrated to each other and to no one else. They recognised how much they needed God in their relationship, to keep them from illicit relationships. How many marriages and engaged couples would benefit from this kind of blessing or prayer between them. Too often, couples today are trying to make a marriage work on their own, independent of God. But as He ordained man to leave his father and his mother and be joined to one woman (Genesis 2:24), God has a better understanding than of any of us, how to keep the three-stranded cord from breaking (Ecclesiastes 4:12).

Engagement today is not seen in the same light as it was then. To the Jewish couple who were receiving this blessing, they would have a full understanding of the expectation being placed upon them – the full implication of God's command regarding illicit relations, because even though they were "only betrothed" they were in a covenant with one another, and the same laws of marriage applied to them as much as if they had consummated their relationship already. The Jewish betrothed couple were to maintain their purity. Remaining holy, just as the Lord has made them holy, as He Himself is holy.

It is interesting to note here the Jewish *Shabbat* (Sabbath) – from sundown on Friday evening, to sundown on Saturday evening. This is a day which is "sanctified" – or set-apart – from the rest of the week, in honour of God's command to keep the seventh day holy (Exodus 20:8-11). Every week, at the *Shabbat* meal, the family gathers together around the table, and welcomes in the Sabbath by reciting the "*Kiddush*"– a blessing over the *Kiddush* Cup of Wine. This cup is then passed around the table for everyone to drink from. I cannot help but notice the similarities between the weekly *Kiddush* and the *Kiddushin* betrothal; nor of the understanding that both the weekly *Shabbat*, and the betrothed couple were sanctified, or set apart to God; nor of the blessing over each cup of wine; nor of the sharing of the drink. Each time they drink from the *Kiddush* cup, the Jewish People remind God of His betrothal to them, and the promise He made to redeem them, as they await *HaMashiach* (The Messiah).

The bride and groom would stand under the "*Chuppah*" (meaning covering or protection), a canopy used in both the *Kiddushin* and the *Nisu'in* (the betrothal and marriage ceremony). It is a piece of material stretched over four poles, open on the four sides, and is meant to be a representation of the home the couple will build together. Spiritually, it represents the covering protection of God over the couple, as His consecrated Bride.

Although not married, in the sense of living together or "becoming one" in flesh and spirit, the bride and groom are married in the sense of being totally committed to one another and set apart for each other – and if either party were to break the covenant, they would be treated in the same way as if the couple's marriage had been finalised through the *nisu'in* stage of the ceremony.

God commands us in ***Exodus 20:3-6:*** *"You shall have no other gods before Me. You shall not make for yourself a carved image—any likeness of anything that is in heaven above, or that is in the earth beneath, or that is in the water under the earth; you shall not bow down to them nor serve them. For I, the LORD your God, am a jealous God, visiting the iniquity of the fathers upon the children to the third and fourth generations of those who hate Me, but showing mercy to thousands, to those who love Me and keep My commandments."* God describes Himself as a jealous God, as a husband jealous for His Bride. We are the Bride of Christ. The Jewish People and the Church who accept Jesus as the Messiah; together we are betrothed to Jesus, and await Him for our wedding ceremony. ***2 Corinthians 11:2:*** *"For I am jealous for you with godly jealousy. For I have betrothed you to* *one husband, that I may present you as a chaste virgin to Christ."*

When Jesus initiated the Last Supper with His disciples, He was initiating a Covenant bond with them, and subsequently with us, as we share in the Lord's Supper. ***Matthew 26:27-29:*** *Then He took the cup, and gave thanks, and gave it to them, saying, "Drink from it, all of you. For this is My blood of the new covenant, which is shed for many for the remission of sins. But I say to you, I will not drink of this fruit of the vine from now on until that day when I drink it new with you in My Father's kingdom."*

1 Corinthians 11:25-26: *In the same manner He also took the cup after supper, saying, "This cup is the new covenant in My blood. This do, as often as you drink it, in remembrance of Me." For as often as you eat this bread and drink this cup, you proclaim the Lord's death till He comes.*

Often these words are "recited" as a blessing over the cup of Communion, and serve as a reminder of what we are partaking in. This is what I see as our *kiddushin* ceremony, each time we take Communion. Why do I say this? Let me show you.

In the Old Testament, we read how God established the Passover Meal (Exodus 12), as part of the relationship between the Israelites and Himself. The Passover Meal was to serve as a reminder to the Jewish People of how God had saved them out of bondage and slavery and brought them to the Promised Land. Jesus was sharing the Passover Meal with His disciples on the night before He was betrayed by one of them. It was a significant Meal between them, and was to become even more significant by what Jesus was about to do.

One of the defining features of the Passover was

setting apart a lamb – one for the whole household. The lamb was to be *"without blemish, a male of the first year. You may take it from the sheep or from the goats. Now you shall keep it until the fourteenth day of the same month. Then the whole assembly of the congregation of Israel shall kill it at twilight."* (Exodus 12:5-6)

The lamb was to be set aside from sunset of the 10th day of the Jewish month of Nisan, and sacrificed on the fourteenth day, but none of the bones of the lamb were to be broken – it was to be kept whole, and roasted whole when being prepared for consumption. It served as a sacrifice for everyone in the house, as God passed over the homes of the children of Israel. The sign of the lamb's blood on the doorposts of each home meant the angel of the Lord did not harm the occupants of that house. Without the sign of the blood, the angel of death struck the household, killing the firstborn son of every home.

The sign of the blood of the sacrificial lamb was the point of salvation for God's chosen people, as He prepared to take them out of Egypt into the Promised Land.

Jesus is the Lamb of God, so by instigating the Last Supper during the Passover Feast, He was identifying Himself with all that the Jewish People would have understood significant about the special sacrifice. For it is only through the blood of the Lamb of God that we are saved from death – not just of the firstborn, this time, but eternal death faced by everyone on the Day of Judgement. John 19:14, 31, 42 (the fact it is mentioned so many times, indicates to me that John is trying to make the point clear!) tells us that the day of Jesus' death coincided with the Day of Preparation – the day of the preparation of the Passover lamb; the day that the Lamb of God died, was the day when the Passover lamb was sacrificed. And just as no bones were broken on the Passover lamb, no bones were broken when the Lamb of God died (John 19:31-33).[5]

Jesus knew what He was about to endure, so it is interesting to note what He tells His disciples in Matthew 26:29: *"But I say to you, I will not drink of this fruit of the vine from now on until that day when I drink it new with you in My Father's kingdom."* What is the significance of this statement?

During the Passover meal, four cups of wine are drunk throughout the course of the meal – each representing a different blessing over the Jewish People. The Last Supper is initiated by Jesus, at the moment of the third cup – leaving the fourth cup to be drunk when He drinks it "new with you in My Father's Kingdom." Jesus is basically telling us He will drink the fourth cup, when He returns to collect His Bride. Then He will drink the marriage cup with her – with us.

But why are four cups of the vine drunk during Passover, and what do the cups represent? A read through the *Haggadah* (literally meaning "telling"; it is the Jewish manuscript and the traditional order for the Passover Meal),[6] identifies how they signify the four "I will" statements made by God as recorded in ***Exodus 6:6-7:*** *"Therefore say to the children of Israel: 'I* am *the Lord;* ***I will bring you out*** *from under the burdens of the Egyptians,* ***I will rescue you*** *from their bondage, and* ***I will redeem you*** *with an outstretched arm and with great judgments.*

'I will take you as My people, and I will be your God*. Then you shall know that I* **am** *the Lord your God who brings you out from under the burdens of the Egyptians.'"* (Emphasis is author's own).

As the Lord spoke these words to Moses, He revealed

the plan by which He would redeem the children of Israel. In a prophetic sense, God was also revealing how He would redeem His elect to become His children. Based on the four promises in the passage above we have the four cups of the Passover feast.

- **The Cup of Sanctification** – "I will bring you out from under the burdens of the Egyptians"
- **The Cup of Judgment or Deliverance** – "I will deliver you from slavery to them"
- **The Cup of Redemption** – "I will redeem you with an outstretched arm"
- **The Cup of Praise or Restoration** – "I will take you to be my people, and I will be your God"

The first cup, the Cup of Sanctification, forms part of the *Kiddushin*. God promised that He would bring His people out from under the cruel oppression of the Egyptians, which parallels God's promise of redemption to His elect through faith in the Son, our Lord Jesus Christ.[7]

Jesus pauses at the third cup, the Cup of Redemption, just before He is about to become our sacrifice of redemption, that through His blood, we will be redeemed to God in His righteousness.

In chapter three, we paused on Jesus' words when He prayed in the Garden of Gethsemane, just before He was betrayed and arrested; as He earnestly asked God to "take the cup" from Him (Matthew 26:39-44). The cup here could have referred to the cup of betrothal, as Jesus knew He was about to pay the bride price for His new Bride-to-be. By drinking from the cup of betrothal, Yeshua was establishing Himself as the covenant Groom. He submits Himself to the purposes of God – for the sake of His people.

When He returns, Jesus will drink of the final cup –

the Cup of Praise or Restoration, when He restores His Bride to Himself. And what a day of great praise and celebration that will be!

Through the Last Supper, Jesus is establishing with us a reminder of the Covenant we have agreed with Him, as our betrothed. He states to His disciples, passed on to the Church through Paul's first letter to Corinth, that when we drink from the cup, we are drinking in accordance with the New Covenant – the New Covenant which incorporates Gentiles as well as the Jewish People.

The Old Covenant God had established was about to be fulfilled through Jesus – the Old Covenant which demanded the sacrificial bride price Jesus had agreed to pay. Through His death and resurrection, Jesus brought in the New Covenant between God and His people, and the New Covenant would allow man to draw close to God in a new way. This is what we partake in when we "eat the bread and drink the wine." The acceptance from us, to enter into the Holy Place with God, and have Him write His laws on our hearts and minds (Hebrews 10:16). Rather than having anyone teach us about how to live, when we abide in Christ, the Spirit Himself will teach us directly concerning how to live in all situations (1 John 2:27).

Just as the Jewish people remind God of His covenant with them every time they share the *Shabbat Kiddish*, the covenant relationship we are in with Jesus is regularly proclaimed and demonstrated by us, every time we partake in Communion.[8] Wow! Who'd have thought that when we eat the bread and drink the cup, we are actually reminding the Lord of the contract we have with Him as His betrothed Bride, as much as we are reminding ourselves that our Beloved Jesus has paid the price for us to be in this wonderful covenant relationship with Him!

Chapter Five

Jewish Wedding Customs – Separated

Now that the couple were formally betrothed to one another, the groom was expected to return to his father's house and prepare a home for his bride during a year of separation.

Before He was arrested by the soldiers, Jesus told His listeners, including you and I who read the Scriptures today, in ***John 14:2-3 (NLT):*** *"There is more than enough room in my Father's home. If this were not so, would I have told you that I am going to prepare a place for you? When everything is ready, I will come and get you, so that you will always be with me where I am."*

And later He reiterates this when He says in ***John 14:28:*** *"You have heard Me say to you, 'I am going away and coming back to you.'"*

As we read, the betrothal of the bride to the groom was followed by the groom leaving her. The betrothal was much more than the engagement we are accustomed to today in the West – I don't think I could have handled Mark asking me to marry him, then disappearing for a whole year! The betrothal was a legally binding agreement, under a *chuppah* in front of the fathers of both parties, and often in front of the High Priest. The couple's names were written in a book and kept, in much the same way we sign the Marriage Register today, with both the Church and the State records.

The newly betrothed couple now underwent a period of separation. This would allow the bride to prepare herself, and allowed the groom to prepare the marital home where the couple would live once their marriage was finalised.

Just as the Jewish bride didn't know when to expect her betrothed husband, we do not know when the Bridegroom will return for His Bride. The Jewish bride would have had an idea, because the betrothal period was for a specific time – a minimum of twelve months. After that time-frame, the groom could return at any time. The bride was expected to await his return and be ready to go at a moment's notice.

Would she need a year to prepare herself? I hear you ask. Good question. I believe a year was the right amount of time for her to make herself ready. If it was good enough for Queen Esther (Esther 2:12), then it was good enough for every Jewish girl to take twelve months to make herself ready. There was a lot for her to do, which we will look at in more detail later.

After the allotted time, she would be alert, watching for the signs of his return for her, because she would have experienced other family or friends' weddings in the past and so would know what to expect. And as she was growing up, she would have been regaled with stories of her father's return for her mother, and received instruction from the older women around her, on what she should look for, and how she should be ready to become a wife. Bear in mind she would have had no "Royal Mail", no phones or mobiles for texting, no video-calling… The bride-to-be only had the memory of the *Kiddushin* to hold on to, and the *Shtar Tena'im* document, created between the bride's father and her groom, and held by her a bit like the Bible is our

Shtar Tena'im, drawn up between God and us.
Matthew 24:42-44: *"Watch therefore, for you do not know what hour your Lord is coming. But know this, that if the master of the house had known what hour the thief would come, he would have watched and not allowed his house to be broken into. Therefore you also be ready, for the Son of Man is coming at an hour you do not expect."*
1 Thessalonians 5:1-2 (NLT): *Now concerning how and when all this will happen, dear brothers and sisters, we don't really need to write you. For you know quite well that the day of the Lord's return will come unexpectedly, like a thief in the night.*
2 Peter 3:10-11: *But the day of the Lord will come as a thief in the night, in which the heavens will pass away with a great noise, and the elements will melt with fervent heat; both the earth and the works that are in it will be burned up. Therefore, since all these things will be dissolved, what manner of persons ought you to be in holy conduct and godliness.*
Revelation 3:3: *"Remember therefore how you have received and heard; hold fast and repent. Therefore if you will not watch, I will come upon you as a thief, and you will not know what hour I will come upon you."*

In the same way, we do not know when Jesus will return for His Church, but we know He will. As we await His return, we need to take heed of Peter's advice (referenced above). There must be times in our life when we would benefit from asking ourselves the question, *what manner of persons ought you to be in holy conduct and godliness.*

As she waited for the groom, the bride-to-be would have checked her conduct – especially around other men. We too, as we await the return of Jesus, should check

our conduct – especially in relation to the things of the world, which can so easily ensnare us.
1 Corinthians 7:23: *God paid a high price for you, so don't be enslaved by the world.* We need to constantly check we are controlled by the Spirit of God, not by our own sinful nature (1 Corinthians 3:3), obeying God and not the devil (Ephesians 2:2), immersed in Him and His ways which are higher than ours (Isaiah 55:9), rather than on the *empty philosophies and high-sounding nonsense that come from human thinking and from the spiritual powers of this world* (Colossians 2:8), laying aside the lusts of the flesh, and putting on the new man of Jesus. In fact, *We should live in this evil world with wisdom, righteousness, and devotion to God, while we look forward with hope to that wonderful day when the glory of our great God and Saviour, Jesus Christ, will be revealed* (Titus 2:12-13).

There is so much instruction in the Word of God for us, that we don't really have any reason to be caught unawares, as if our home is being ransacked by a thief in the night. Jesus has told us what will happen, and He has told us the signs which will indicate His return. There is a specific time allotted for Jesus to be away from His Bride, determined by The Father; we are to watch for the signs indicating Yeshua is on His way to collect us and take us home to His Father's house.
Matthew 24:3-14: *Now as He sat on the Mount of Olives, the disciples came to Him privately, saying, "Tell us, when will these things be? And what will be the sign of Your coming, and of the end of the age?" And Jesus answered and said to them: "Take heed that no one deceives you. For many will come in My name, saying, 'I am the Christ,' and will deceive many. And you will hear of wars and rumours of wars. See that you are not*

troubled; for all these things must come to pass, but the end is not yet. For nation will rise against nation, and kingdom against kingdom. And there will be famines, pestilences, and earthquakes in various places. All these are the beginning of sorrows. Then they will deliver you up to tribulation and kill you, and you will be hated by all nations for My name's sake. And then many will be offended, will betray one another, and will hate one another. Then many false prophets will rise up and deceive many. And because lawlessness will abound, the love of many will grow cold. But he who endures to the end shall be saved. And this gospel of the kingdom will be preached in all the world as a witness to all the nations, and then the end will come."

If you look around you today, you will see there are many of the signs Jesus spoke about, which seem as though they are becoming more and more visible. There are wars. There are rumours, or threats of wars, as one nation rises against another. There are famines across whole countries. We've seen increases of "pestilences" or fatal, incurable diseases. And there has been what feels like an awakening of the earth, as shown by the increase of earthquakes – in intensity, as well as in quantity. Christians around the world are being persecuted for their belief in Jesus as Lord, even in the 21st Century, and even within the UK. You have only to tune in to some television debates or read the news to hear of Christians being sued because they chose to stand by their beliefs, or people being fired from work because of their faith in God. This is because *everybody is doing what is right in their own eyes* (Judges 21:25) and as the rights of some minority groups in society become worth more than the traditional values of the Word of God. It is also because, quite frankly, *lawlessness abounds*.

I could go on, as we hear of people calling themselves "God's Prophet So-and-So" or "Chosen Apostle Whoever" trying to tell the Church their way is the only way, and their interpretation of religion and the Scriptures is the *only* one to follow if you really want to get to heaven. For example, many will have heard of self-styled "messiah" Michael Travesser (Wayne Bent) who predicted the end of the world would occur in October 2007; he was the subject of a Channel 4 investigative documentary, *The End of the World Cult*.[9] He tried to convince his followers he was given the title of "messiah", when God "spoke" with him in his living room in the year 2000. He was arrested and convicted of sexual crimes against minors and contributing to the delinquency of a minor. The only Scripture he fulfilled was Matthew 7:15: "Beware of false prophets, who come to you in sheep's clothing, but inwardly they are ravenous wolves." And Matthew 24:24: "For false christs and false prophets will rise and show great signs and wonders to deceive, if possible, even the elect." At the time of writing, there were newspaper reports of a cult claiming that the world would end in June 2012. They were known as Growing in Grace International. I think the fact you are reading this after June 2012 speaks for itself of the falseness of this particular prophecy and the claims of the self-styled leader! The leader has called himself "the antichrist" and enforces his followers to have a tattoo to match his – the number 666. He rejects "the Jewish teachings of Jesus", accepting for study instead the teachings of the Apostle Paul, with whom he claims to be in direct contact.[10]

Jude 3-4: *... **contend earnestly for the faith** which was once for all delivered to the saints. **For certain men have crept in unnoticed**, who long ago were marked* *out for this condemnation, ungodly men, who turn the grace of our God into lewdness and deny the only Lord God and our Lord Jesus Christ...* (Emphasis is author's own). But the heart of the Bride is relentless toward her soon-coming Groom, as the Lord's people hold on to Him, preaching His truth – that Jesus Christ is the *only* way to the Father. And so the *"gospel of the kingdom will be preached in all the world"* (Matthew 24:14).

Though we are close, we are so very close, do not be deceived. Do not allow yourself to be led astray from the truth of the love Jesus has for you. Do not allow anyone to lie to you and pull you away from the heart of your soon-coming Groom. Do not allow anyone to deceive you into thinking He is not coming, or that He has come in another form. Stay alert. Keep watching, expectantly. Yeshua hasn't forgotten His promise to His Bride.

1 Thessalonians 5:4-6: *But you, brethren, are not in darkness, so that this Day should overtake you as a thief. You are all sons of light and sons of the day. We are not of the night nor of darkness. Therefore let us not sleep, as others do, but let us watch and be sober.*

As well as looking out for the signs of Jesus' return, it is important we don't let anyone distract us or deceive us into following after someone who is not our Lord, and causing us to break our Covenant with Him. Just as a woman, if she is told her betrothed is dead, may – after a respectable period of mourning – start to look for a new man who will marry her. In the same way, many throughout history have tried to convince Jesus' Bride that He has died and will not be coming back for her. Church, hold on... He is not dead – He is alive! And He is coming soon to claim you to Himself once again. The wedding feast is almost ready – ***Isaiah 25:6 (NLT):*** *"In Jerusalem, the LORD of Heaven's Armies will spread a* *wonderful feast for all the people of the world. It will be a delicious banquet with clear, well-aged wine and choice meat."*

Don't lose heart and don't give up – keep watching, keep waiting, you shall surely soon see Him!

Matthew 24:4: *"Take heed that no one deceives you."*

2 John 1:7: *For many deceivers have gone out into the world who do not confess Jesus Christ as coming in the flesh. This is a deceiver and an antichrist.*

2 Thessalonians 2:1-4: *Now, brethren, concerning the coming of our Lord Jesus Christ and our gathering together to Him, we ask you, not to be soon shaken in mind or troubled, either by spirit or by word or by letter, as if from us, as though the day of Christ had come. Let no one deceive you by any means; for that Day will not come unless the falling away comes first, and the man of sin is revealed, the son of perdition, who opposes and exalts himself above all that is called God or that is worshiped, so that he sits as God in the temple of God, showing himself that he is God.*

Is satan real? Is he really out to deceive the Church, to keep her away from her Beloved? Is he really trying to hinder you from being ready for the greatest wedding day you will ever attend? You'd better believe it! He is very definitely hard at work trying to deceive Jesus' Bride, with his army of fallen angels, every minute of every day! But sadly, many Christians do not believe it!

God warns us through Paul's second letter to the Corinthians of what satan is like, ***2 Corinthians 11:14:*** *And no wonder! For satan himself transforms himself into an angel of light.*

Now if you, for whatever reason, wanted to see something "outside" of the infallible Word of God to believe in the existence and activity of satan, please understand that there are people, in times both past and present, who have it in mind to purposely deceive God's people about him. They proclaim false reports about him, trying to show believers the opposite of what God's Word says, calling evil good, and good evil (Isaiah 5:20). We are seeing this being played out more and more, as sexual immorality is applauded while sexual modesty is ridiculed. Drug-takers are honoured, whilst those who live a holy life are laughed at. The things of the darkness are being opened up, while the things of the "Light" (that is, the things of Christ, who is the Light of the world) are being hidden away. This is why it is so important for us, as believers, to "test all things" (1 Thessalonians 5:21) and to "test every spirit" (1 John 4:1).

The Bible describes satan as the god of this age, ***2 Corinthians 4:4:*** *whose minds the god of this age has blinded.* And it is clear, as the Light of Christ shines on it, how the domination of the god of this age is blinding the minds and hearts of men and women all over the world, to the truth of the Messiah. We see this in children's cartoons which are based on demonic-looking characters who "take over" the body/mind/spirit of the hero with "special" powers; music videos which are overtly sexualised or pagan-ritualistic; films and television programmes which glorify violence, death, reincarnation and immortality, rather than life and love; society's acceptance of anything and everything which goes against God's Word and against His laws, but a total rejection of God Himself. Things which were once seen as evil are becoming celebrated, whilst those things which were once deemed moral are being ridiculed and frowned upon.

It is clear that the god of this age has an agenda. As we draw closer to the return of the Bridegroom for His

Bride, we see it intensifying as it tries to distract the Bride from keeping a look out for her Groom. You have only to switch on the television for a few minutes to see how the media has become a vessel for the agenda of the god of this age, and the speed with which it is spreading and intensifying. He rules the world, and is trying to rule God's people, and the Church. We need to recognise the signs, be aware of our enemy the devil, for he prowls around like a roaring lion, looking to divide and conquer, looking to devour the Bride of Yeshua (1 Peter 5:8).

Romans 1:20-32: *For since the creation of the world His invisible attributes are clearly seen, being understood by the things that are made, even His eternal power and Godhead, so that they are without excuse, because, although they knew God, they did not glorify Him as God, nor were thankful, but became futile in their thoughts, and their foolish hearts were darkened. Professing to be wise, they became fools, and changed the glory of the incorruptible God into an image made like corruptible man – and birds and four-footed animals and creeping things. Therefore God also gave them up to uncleanness, in the lusts of their hearts, to dishonour their bodies among themselves,* ***who exchanged the truth of God for the lie****, and* ***worshiped and served the creature rather than the Creator****, who is blessed forever. Amen. For this reason God gave them up to vile passions. For even their women exchanged the natural use for what is against nature. Likewise also the men, leaving the natural use of the woman, burned in their lust for one another, men with men committing what is shameful, and receiving in themselves the penalty of their error which was due. And even as they did not like to retain God in their knowledge, God gave them over to a debased mind, to do those things which are* *not fitting;* ***being filled with all unrighteousness, sexual immorality, wickedness, covetousness, maliciousness; full of envy, murder, strife, deceit, evil-mindedness; they are whisperers, backbiters, haters of God, violent, proud, boasters, inventors of evil things, disobedient to parents, undiscerning, untrustworthy, unloving, unforgiving, unmerciful; who, knowing the righteous judgment of God****, that those who practice such things are deserving of death, not only do the same but* ***also approve of those who practice them***. (Emphasis is author's own.)

We see how the agenda of the god of this age remains the same, but the way it outplays itself varies, depending on what is "acceptable" to each nation.

In Western culture, we have the exaltation of money and celebrity status, both within the secular and Christian markets, as people are idolised above God, and worship is directed away from *Adonai*, the Most Holy, towards dust-created men and women. In parts of South America and Africa, demon-worship is more overtly prevalent as witch-doctors are sought out. While in China or North Korea, for example, individuals don't "exist" as people are seen by the state as a faceless mass, unified in what they are told, and how they are warned life should be lived. And that's without mentioning other religions and idolatry, which are all used to draw the Bride away from her Groom.

Mark and I went on a cruise around the Mediterranean for our honeymoon, which was such an experience. One of the countries we visited was Turkey, stopping off in two different cities. In one of the places, I was aware of such heaviness, I couldn't handle walking around the City. There was such a spiritual oppression, and as we made our way back to the liner, the sheer number of idols, and "Evil Eye" Talismans was overwhelming.

Isaiah 26:10 (NLT): *"O LORD our God, others have ruled us, but you alone are the one we worship."*

But the god of this age hasn't only just started to work out his agenda, he has always been "behind the scenes" as it were, trying to seduce the Bride of Christ and draw her attention towards him, instead of toward Yeshua, weakening the nations (Isaiah 14:12). Using the same tricks and methods as he has over time, he is waiting for the time to ensnare God's creation away from the pure love found in our Heavenly Father.

An example of this purposeful determination to deceive dates back to 1872. Albert Pike, Sovereign Grand Commander of the Scottish Rite of Freemasonry's Southern Jurisdiction (1859 to 1891), was the most powerful Freemason in America. He published a book, *Morals and Dogma of the Ancient and Accepted Scottish Rite of Freemasonry* in which he candidly states the following: "Lucifer, the light-bearer! Strange and mysterious name to give to the **spirit of darkness**! Lucifer, the son of the morning! **Is it he** who bears the light, and with its splendours intolerable **blinds feeble, sensual or selfish souls? Doubt it not!**"[11] (Emphasis is author's own.)

It is funny (peculiar) to see how the "spirit of darkness" is being likened to being the bearer of light, especially as darkness and light cannot work together, for where the light shines, darkness has to flee away. When you enter a darkened room, as soon as you switch on the light, darkness is dispelled, hiding in the shadows ready to spring out again once the light is removed. How, then, can the created "prince of darkness" actually be the bearer of light? Wake up and recognise the *true Light*, the Bridegroom, Yeshua, our Jesus!

If the deception is not in trying to hide the reality of his existence (for many in the world doubt the existence of satan), it's in the way satan and his followers try to show him as being the complete opposite of what he really is. Yes the Bible says Lucifer was once the morning star,[12] but this was before he was thrown out of heaven. It is satan who Jesus defeated at the cross. It is he who blinds the eyes and minds of mankind to the Truth contained within Jesus Christ.

From 2 Peter 3:3-4, we see how satan has wrongfully been trying to convince the Church that Jesus will never return, ever since Jesus ascended into heaven: *"... for scoffers will come in the last days and saying, 'Where is the promise of His coming?' For since the fathers fell asleep, all things continue as they were from the beginning of creation."* He is trying to convince the Jews that the Messiah will never come for them, never mind that Yeshua, the Messiah has already been, and trying to convince the world that today is all that counts, for there is nothing after death. All around us, we can see how many of the people we know have succumbed to this erroneous teaching, this most evil of all deceptions! But we are to remember that ... *the Lord is not slack concerning His promise... But the Day of the Lord will come as a thief in the night.* (2 Peter 3:9-10)

God will not force His way into our hearts, nor will He make us behave in the appropriate way. The choice of whom we serve is ours.

Ezekiel 14:3: *"Son of man, these men have set up their idols in their hearts, and put before them that which causes them to stumble into iniquity. Should I let Myself be inquired of at all by them?"*

Who – or what – have you set up in your heart? Church, stop sleeping and wake up! Be aware – your enemy the devil is prowling around trying to devour you, trying to deceive you, trying to hinder you from enjoying the fullness of eternal life with Jesus, your Beloved.

We are urged to live as the Jewish bride lived, as she waited for her groom to arrive for her. We are to live our lives in total devotion to our Groom, as though He was just around the corner, not as though we are of the world and alienated from Him.

Ephesians 4:17-24: *This I say, therefore, and testify in the Lord, that you should no longer walk as the rest of the Gentiles walk, in the futility of their mind, having their understanding darkened, being alienated from the life of God, because of the ignorance that is in them, because of the blindness of their heart; who, being past feeling, have given themselves over to lewdness, to work all uncleanness with greediness.*

Philippians 1:27: *Only let your conduct be worthy of the gospel of Christ…*

We have learned a different way in the life and teaching of Yeshua, a new way of living in righteousness and holiness.

1 Thessalonians 4:1-8 (NLT): *Finally, dear brothers and sisters, we urge you in the name of the Lord Jesus to live in a way that pleases God … God's will is for you to be holy, so stay away from all sexual sin. Then each of you will control his own body and live in holiness and honour— not in lustful passion like the pagans who do not know God and his ways. … God has called us to live holy lives, not impure lives. Therefore, anyone who refuses to live by these rules is not disobeying human teaching but is rejecting God, who gives his Holy Spirit to you.*

The ways of the world are glamorised and made to look appealing, but the truth is they are destructive –

I'm not just talking about sexual immorality here, but all aspects of what appeals to the flesh, or the old man, is destructive to the body, mind and, more importantly, to the spirit. And to what end? The god of this age is fighting a battle he has already lost – and his agenda is to take you into the pit of hell with him. The place which is marked with his name after Jesus returns for His Bride, is not the place God has marked for you for eternity. But, the Gentleman that God is, He will not force His ways upon you. Unlike satan.

Revelation 19:20: *"Then the beast was captured, and with him the false prophet who worked signs in his presence, by which he deceived those who received the mark of the beast and those who worshiped his image."*

Friends! Wake up to the Truth! Then shout and proclaim the Truth to your neighbours! We need to encourage one another, support each other, and exhort those around us on the narrow path of Truth (Hebrews 10:24-25). We should be lifting others up when they stumble, drawing them into the holy of holies with God daily, reminding each other that Jesus is the Truth! And the Truth is the Groom *will* return for His Bride. Jesus is coming back for His people! Amen!

This is all part of our preparation. This is what it means for us to get ready. The days we are living in are the last days. These days are crucial, and we have limited time to get ready! Just as a bride will do all she can to get ready for her wedding day, we have to do all we can to make ourselves ready for Jesus' return! And just as a bride has very limited time to get ready on the day of her wedding, our time is now very limited.

Chapter Six

Jewish Wedding Customs – Pre-Wedding Preparation

As we continue to look through the Jewish customs of Jesus' day, we move away from the initial betrothal, to the period of preparation. We know what the groom is doing as he prepares himself to come and get his bride, so what is the bride doing?

Throughout their time of separation, the bride-to-be will spend the time preparing for life beyond the wedding, as well as for the day itself, including fashioning her bridal outfit.

Before she can get dressed in her fine wedding garments, the bride has to make herself ready inside and out. She would receive training from her elders on how to be a wife, how to manage her household and how to look after her husband's needs physically, emotionally and sexually. She would be provided with fine oils and perfumes – as Queen Esther had been in times past (Esther 2:12-13).

In the Old Testament book of Ruth, we read how Ruth was told by Naomi to prepare herself, before she went out to speak to Boaz, ***Ruth 3:3:*** *"Therefore wash yourself and anoint yourself, put on your best garment and go down to the threshing floor…"* – this command also applies to the future Bride of Yeshua. This is all part of what it means for us to "get ready"!

Being washed – in the blood of Jesus; by repenting from

our sins, and being baptised in water.
Being perfumed – with the "oil" of the Holy Spirit.
Being dressed in our best garments – our Robes of Righteousness.

1 Corinthians 6:11: *And such were some of you. But you were washed, but you were sanctified, but you were justified in the name of the Lord Jesus and by the Spirit of our God.*

Ephesians 5:2: *And walk in love, as Christ also has loved us and given Himself for us, an offering and a sacrifice to God for a sweet-smelling aroma.*

Song of Solomon 4:10: *"Your love delights me, my treasure, my bride. Your love is better than wine, your perfume more fragrant than spices."*

Zechariah 3:4: *Then He answered and spoke to those who stood before Him, saying, "Take away the filthy garments from him." And to him He said, "See, I have removed your iniquity from you, and I will clothe you with rich robes."*

When we are washed and anointed from the inside out, the person we were before Jesus, begins to give way to the person God is transforming us into — a better version of who we once were. Walking in light, rather than darkness, walking in hope rather than fear; walking in love, rather than hatred, walking in joy, rather than despondency; walking in peace, rather than discontent; walking in patience, rather than impatience and frustration; extending kindness, above selfish ambition; walking in goodness, rather than in evil; demonstrating faithfulness, rather than wanton wandering; speaking with gentleness, rather than harshness; walking with self-control, rather than impulsive behaviour – the old man giving way to the new man.

These are ways in which we are able to prepare

ourselves for the return of our Groom. And as a bride begins to reflect the love of her life, we begin to reflect our Lord, as our hearts give way to the transforming power of His Holy Spirit.

The bride-to-be will also spend time preparing herself emotionally and mentally for becoming a wife. She will need to re-learn some old habits – particularly if she has lived on her own for a while. She will need to learn what it will take for her to be a wife, to have someone always there with her, submitting to him, allowing herself to step back from making all the decisions alone, and seek out her husband's advice or opinion. Learning how to respond to him, how to speak with him, how to open her heart to him – even in the difficult moments when she would rather hide away by herself. Learning who her husband is: his dreams, his hopes and aspirations, and how to help him achieve these, drawing the best out of him, so they can achieve the dream together.

Genesis 2:18; 21-22 (AMP): *Now the Lord God said, It is not good (sufficient, satisfactory) that the man should be alone; I will make him a helper meet (**suitable, adapted, complementary**) for him... And the Lord God caused a deep sleep to fall upon Adam; and while he slept, He took one of his ribs or a part of his side and closed up the [place with] flesh. And the rib or part of his side which the Lord God had taken from the man He built up and made into a woman, and He brought her to the man.* (Emphasis is author's own.)

Ephesians 5:22 (AMP): *Wives, be subject (be submissive and adapt yourselves) to your own husbands as [a service] to the Lord.*

Colossians 3:18 (AMP): *Wives, be subject to your husbands [subordinate and adapt yourselves to them], as is right and fitting and your proper duty in the Lord.*

How does this relate to the Bride of Christ? Surely these verses are only relevant for an individual wife to her individual husband? Maybe, but look closely at one of the sentences Paul writes, as he continues his instruction to the marriage relationship.

Ephesians 5:24 (NLT): *As the church submits to Christ, so you wives should submit to your husbands in everything*. (Emphasis is author's own.)

As the Church submits to Christ – there it is. The Church is compared with the wife. We need to submit ourselves to Jesus, as much as a wife does to her husband. How often do we actually submit ourselves to Him in our daily lives, or in our corporate times of worship? There was a scary thing I have heard a number of times over the years, that should God remove the Holy Spirit from the Church, most people would not notice. I pray this is not true of us!

Part of the work of the Holy Spirit within us, as He prepares us for the coming of our Lord, is to cleanse us, transform us and renew us.

If we look back at what is being undertaken by a young woman – or man – preparing for marriage, there will be certain kinds of behaviour she will stop doing, now she is betrothed, things she may have done whilst single, in order to try to attract a mate, places she would have visited in order to catch a man's eye. She will learn what it means to be transformed from being a single woman to becoming married.

Before I met Mark, although I spent a lot of time with my female friends, I wouldn't think twice about hanging out with some of my male friends too. But when I decided to commit to the relationship and my future with Mark, I chose to not spend time one-on-one with any of my male friends. I had to change the way I perceived this "hanging out" with them; to see it from Mark's perspective as the one I had chosen to accept as my future husband, changing my thinking from "singleton" to "married". After all, how would I feel if Mark decided to spend time one-on-one with another female?

In the same way, we long to please our soon-coming Groom with our actions, with the choices we make and the way we live each day. We try to love Him with all our heart, all our mind, and all soul. We long to be pure before Him, cleansed from all unrighteousness, to be holy, as He is holy, so that when we stand before Him, He will draw us unto Himself and not reject us. Out of our genuine love for our God, we choose to do the things which demonstrate our love for Him. Our mind-set has to change from the way of the world, to the way of the Kingdom of God. It is hard, because we have been living according to the world's way for so long, but if our hearts are right before Him, and as a groom knows his bride-to-be, our Jesus knows us – He understands that that we have tried our best to run the race set before us (Hebrews 12:1) as we tried to live for Him.

As an engaged couple delight in each other, Jesus wants us to delight in Him as much as He delights in us. When they are first engaged, a couple tend to spend a lot of time with each other, drinking in as much information about the one they have chosen, as they can – talking for hours as wedding plans are made, and future dreams are discussed. Jesus wants to show you how much He delights in you, in this same way, through the time you spend with Him, through the hours you talk with Him.

But beyond that, demonstrating our love for our betrothed means keeping our bodies for them, and our minds fixed on the life we will have with them. When

I was engaged to Mark I did not allow any thoughts of another man to enter into my mind (and, of course, since being married to him the same has been true). Other friends may discuss which male actor/singer/sportsman they find attractive – or think is good looking – but I have chosen to not entertain this type of thinking. Because I know a thought can become a fixation, and a fixation can lead to sin. As we read in ***James 1:14-15 (NLT):*** *Temptation comes from our own desires, which entice us and drag us away. These desires give birth to sinful actions. And when sin is allowed to grow, it gives birth to death.*

As Mark's fiancée and wife, I chose to present my body undefiled to him on our wedding day. I kept myself pure from sexual sin and on our wedding day, Mark had the confidence in my devotion and love for him on the night of our wedding.

In the same way, Yeshua desires for us to keep our bodies and minds for Him. Not in a sick and twisted kind of a way – which some people in the world would like to have you think – but spiritually, to keep yourself pure from following after other gods or serving other idols. To fix our mind on things above, and not on the things of this world (Colossians 3:2).

Romans 12:1-2: *I beseech you therefore, brethren, by the mercies of God, that* ***you present your bodies a living sacrifice, holy, acceptable to God****, which is your reasonable service. And do not be conformed to this world, but* ***be transformed by the renewing of your mind****, that you may prove what is that good and acceptable and perfect will of God.* (Emphasis is author's own).

1 Thessalonians 4:3-5 (NLT): *God's will is for you to be holy, so stay away from all sexual sin. Then each of* *you will control his own body and live in holiness and honour—not in lustful passion like the pagans who do not know God and his ways.*

Not only will the bride-to-be take time to prepare herself inside and out, with her attitudes, thought-processes, the way her skin looks or the way she smells, but she will also spend a lot of time looking for *the dress*! She wants to look her best for her husband. The clothes she wears are probably one of the most important aspects for her, as she prepares for the wedding.

Many brides have an idea of the kind of dress they want, before her beau has even proposed to her – for some, this means keeping a scrapbook of what she likes, as she grows from child to adult. For others this means having a dress which is a clear reflection of who she is as a woman.

One of my friends asked me to be a bridesmaid for her, and I was amazed when she brought us all together for a celebratory dinner and pulled out a scrapbook of plans and ideas she had collected over the years of her engagement for her wedding, only because I hadn't expected it from her, and yet, I learned a lot from her example!

I, however, was in the latter category. I had a clear idea of what I wanted, and knew it wouldn't be something I would be able to purchase off the shelves, as it was *that* distinct. Or if I could have found it on the shelves, it probably wouldn't have been within my low-budget range!

So I spoke with a dress designer friend of mine who was in the Church I attended at the time, and shared with her the vision of what I wanted, showed her a few cuttings of similar styles which I wanted to incorporate, and the colour – which for me was *the* most important part of the design! Nike went away, drew a few designs based on our discussions and together we agreed on the design, materials, colour and detail of the dress!

As Nike worked on the dress over the months leading up to the day of the wedding, it was a great honour to watch it taking shape. It took time for the dress to be ready – as it takes time for any aspect of the wedding to be ready.

But when it was finished, it was so me. It was so unique. It was perfect. Nike had done a brilliant job at converting ideas from my thoughts on a page to the reality I wore. When I wore it, I felt amazing – as any bride does in her special dress!

But don't be fooled, this is not just for the ladies – my hubby, Mark, was very hands-on with his own outfit too! He had a very clear idea of what he wanted to look like on our wedding day. And so he too hunted around for the right clothes. He particularly wanted to wear a white bow-tie. Not pink to match my outfit, not grey, not black or any other colour, he wanted white – and not a fake one on elastic, no, Mark wanted the real McCoy. He would spend hours looking for one, along with his suit which had to be a particular shade of grey, as similar to the 1930s deco style as he could find! And I have to say – as I walked down the aisle toward him, it paid off – he looked absolutely gorgeous!

In the same way, the clothes the Bride of Christ will wear are just as important, and will take as much time in preparation as they do for any wedding.

Revelation 19:8: *And to her it was granted to be arrayed in fine linen, clean and bright, for the fine linen is the righteous acts of the saints.*

Romans 13: 12-14a (NLT): *The night is almost gone; the day of salvation will soon be here. So remove your* *dark deeds like dirty clothes, and put on the shining armour of right living. Because we belong to the day, we must live decent lives for all to see. Don't participate in the darkness of wild parties and drunkenness, or in sexual promiscuity and immoral living, or in quarrelling and jealousy. Instead, clothe yourself with the presence of the Lord Jesus Christ.*

Colossians 3:12-14 (NLT): *Since God chose you to be the holy people he loves, you must clothe yourselves with tender-hearted mercy, kindness, humility, gentleness, and patience. Make allowance for each other's faults, and forgive anyone who offends you. Remember, the Lord forgave you, so you must forgive others. Above all, clothe yourselves with love, which binds us all together in perfect harmony.*

The end result of all this hard work and preparation for the Bride of Christ?

Spectacular.

Amazing.

Breath-taking.

Awe-inspiring.

Pause, and see for yourself:

Revelation 21:2; 11 (AMP): *And I saw the holy city, the new Jerusalem, descending out of heaven from God, all arrayed like a bride beautified and adorned for her husband... Clothed in God's glory [in all its splendour and radiance]. The lustre of it resembled a rare and most precious jewel, like jasper, shining clear as crystal.*

Psalm 45:7-15 (NLT): *...your God, has anointed you, pouring out the oil of joy on you more than on anyone else. Myrrh, aloes, and cassia perfume your robes... For your royal husband delights in your beauty; honour Him, for He is your Lord... The bride, a princess, looks glorious in her golden gown. In her beautiful robes,* *she is led to the king, accompanied by her bridesmaids. What a joyful and enthusiastic procession as they enter the king's palace!*

Here we have a *selah* moment. Can you hear the sharp intake of breath in heaven, as God's Chosen People; the Old Covenant and the New, the Royal Bride of Yeshua is revealed. Stop a moment and imagine the scene. Wow!

But the pre-wedding preparations don't stop there! The process of preparing extends to the rest of the Bridal Party, the parents of the bride, as well as members of the family who are to be involved in any aspect of the day. Oh, and the rest of the wedding guests! We may not have to clothe everybody, but we do need to prepare everyone for our big day, in providing details of where the ceremony and the following Wedding Breakfast will be held – including maps if necessary, details of where guests can stay overnight – to suit all types of budgets, information of the wedding list if guests require it – along with any other information people will inevitably ask you, as they get ready to join you on the day.

The point is, we don't want anyone we love, are close to, or who we consider family or friend, who we have invited to our wedding, not to be able to make it to the wedding feast for any reason.

In the same way we have a duty as we prepare for the final wedding feast to ensure that both our Christian family who also make up the Bride of Christ, as well as those who are still in the world, yet to be brought into faith in Jesus, are prepared for the Final Day:

Ephesians 4:15-16: *...but, speaking the truth in love, may grow up in all things into Him who is the head— Christ— from whom the whole body, joined and knit together by what every joint supplies, according to the effective working by which every part does its share,*

causes growth of the body for the edifying of itself in love.
Ephesians 5:25-27: *...just as Christ also loved the church and gave Himself for her, that He might sanctify and cleanse her with the washing of water by the word, that He might present her to Himself a glorious church, not having spot or wrinkle or any such thing, but that she should be holy and without blemish.*
2 Timothy 4:1-4: *I charge you therefore before God and the Lord Jesus Christ, who will judge the living and the dead at His appearing and His kingdom:* ***Preach the word!*** *Be ready in season and out of season. Convince, rebuke, exhort, with all longsuffering and teaching. For* ***the time will come when they will not endure sound doctrine****, but according to their own desires, because they have itching ears, they will heap up for themselves teachers; and they will turn their ears away from the truth, and be turned aside to fables. But you be watchful in all things, endure afflictions,* ***do the work of an evangelist, fulfil your ministry****.* (Emphasis is author's own).

Chapter Seven

Jewish Wedding Customs – The Wedding Procession

During their time of separation, the groom was expected to build the marital home within his father's house, ready to bring home his bride – which usually explained the minimum twelve month period, as it takes time to build a house... properly! When it was ready, at his father's command, the groom would go and retrieve his bride. Usually this took place at night, as the groom made his way with his best man, and other attendants, in a joyful torch-light procession to the home of his waiting bride.

The groom would not be able to take the decision himself when the house was ready – most men would have done a quick-job in order to get their wife home quick! Instead, he would have had his work checked by his father.

> [The bridegroom] ... had to get his father's approval before he could consider it ready for his bride. If asked the date of his wedding he would have to reply, "Only my father knows."[13]

This is why we read in Mark 13:32 (and elsewhere) Jesus telling His disciples: *"no one knows the day or hour when these things will happen, not even the angels in heaven or the Son Himself. Only the Father knows."* When He was on earth, Jesus was given authority from the Father to do the things He did. He continues to bring good news to the poor, comfort the broken-hearted, proclaim release for the captives, prisoners are set free, the sick are healed, etc (Isaiah 61:1-3), and Jesus is still at work, preparing a place for us and interceding on our behalf. The Father is the only One who knows when He will send His Son back to receive the Bride being prepared for Him. What a beautiful picture of the harmony of God working for our benefit, always out of the depth of His love for us.

But once the house was prepared, once the home was ready for his wife to complete the work he had started, the groom was ready to go and collect his bride.

According to Jewish tradition, the procession usually started at night for those who were busy during the day so they could attend and celebrate with the happy couple; plus it allowed for a spectacular display of lights and torches, demonstrating the successful prowess of the groom and his family.

"At the sight of the groom's procession, crowds looked down from roof-tops (Song of Solomon 3:11), and the women took up a peculiar cry of wedding joy that told those farther along that the pageant had started. This cry was continued all along the route, and gave warning to those who were waiting with the bride that it was time to arise and light up the approach, and welcome the bridegroom with honour."[14]

The night-time procession, and return of the groom indicated that the bride should be ready at any time of the day or night, for he could return any time he was ready, to collect her "like a thief in the night".

Matthew 24:42-44 (NKJ): *Watch therefore, for you do not know what hour your Lord is coming. But know this, that if the master of the house had known what hour the thief would come, he would have watched and not allowed his house to be broken into. Therefore you also* *be ready, for the Son of Man is coming at an hour you do not expect.*

There have been a number of reports in the news, relating to burglary and the rights of a homeowner over the human rights of the burglar. Nowadays, it seems as though a thief doesn't necessarily need to come 'in the night', to carry out his evil deed, as more and more burglaries are being carried out during the day. But if any of us heard a rumour our home was going to be 'done over' on a particular day, we would probably call everyone around to help us protect our home; we would make sure we were ready for them!

In the same way, Jesus is alerting us to the fact that He will return for His Bride as soon as the place He is preparing is ready for her, at any time of the day or night – although we are certainly in a spiritual 'night'! If we received a word telling us for definite, when Jesus was coming back, we would make every effort to ensure we were alert and ready to meet Him. This is why the enemy has used so many false "prophecies" of people trying to tell the world "Jesus is returning on such and such a date". The more he can prod the boy to cry "wolf", the less people will believe the reports out of sheer irritation with all the previous false reports, and the less people will believe Jesus will return (2 Peter 3:3-4). For many in the Church, the last 2,000 years makes them think that His promise to return and take home His Bride is false – they have given up hope. Just as many Jewish People 2,000 years ago had given up believing the Messiah would come to save them.

Satan tries to convince the Church – and subsequently the world – that God's delay means He isn't going to turn up. Ever since the beginning of time, satan has been asking humanity, "*did God really say…*" (Genesis

3:1), and not just humanity – satan used the same trick to tempt Jesus into sinning too (Luke 4:1-14), by challenging the Word of God and Jesus' authority. And as the Day of the Lord's return approaches, the question *"Did God really say…"* is being asked more and more in an attempt to challenge our understanding of the Word of God and to dissuade us from holding on to the truth. This causes us to look down instead of up, leading us away from watching out for the signs of the return of our Groom. Be alert Church! Be ready!

Zephaniah 1:7: *Be silent in the presence of the Lord God; For the day of the LORD is at hand, For the LORD has prepared a sacrifice; He has invited His guests.*

Ours is *not* to know the day or the hour, our place is just to make sure we are ready and not sleeping, and that those around us are also ready and not sleeping.

As with the waiting bride and her maids, we must have our lamps lit and spare oil by our sides, ready to be taken up at a moment's notice. The bride would keep these items with her veil and dress, in easy reach, so she was ready to go as soon as she heard the shouting through the streets, "He's coming! The Groom is on his way!"

Jesus' parable of the ten virgins also demonstrates for us, the responsibility that is on every member of the Wedding Party. He warns us personally how we need to ensure we are ready to go, to be a part of the Wedding Procession when the Bridegroom arrives to claim His Bride.

Matthew 25:6-10: *"And at midnight a cry was heard: 'Behold, the bridegroom is coming; go out to meet him!' Then all those virgins arose and trimmed their lamps. And the foolish said to the wise, 'Give us some of your oil, for our lamps are going out.' But the wise answered, saying, 'No, lest there should not be enough* *for us and you; but go rather to those who sell, and buy for yourselves.' And while they went to buy, the bridegroom came, and those who were ready went in with him..."*

Let's look in a little more detail at the significance of the lamps and the oil they held, at what Jesus is trying to teach us in this parable – at what He is warning, and how He is advising us.

The Lamp

What does "the lamp" symbolise? Using the Bible as our resource to fully understand what Jesus is teaching us, we can see two distinct aspects of what the lamp represents.

The dictionary definition for a lamp is, "Any vessel which is used for illumination, often through the use of a wick dipped in oil". The Bible often speaks of a lamp and, I believe, it represents the illumination in our lives, through the direction of the Holy Spirit, through following God's laws and statutes, or through reading His Word (see Psalm 119:105).

We are created as spiritual beings as well as physical creatures and the Bible often describes our lives as being lamps through which the Light can shine out to a dark and desperate world.

In ***Matthew 5:15-16***, Jesus said, *"Nor do they light a lamp and put it under a basket, but on a lampstand, and it gives light to all who are in the house. Let your light so shine before men, that they may see your good works and glorify your Father in heaven."*

The physical body we have been given is a clay vessel for the spiritual part of who we are, through whom God is able to illuminate our spirit – either to illuminate our own heart's condition or to illuminate the situation around us for other people.

Proverbs 20:27: *The spirit of a man is* ***the lamp of the Lord****, searching all the inner depths of his heart.* (Emphasis is author's own.)

2 Corinthians 4:6-7: *For it is the God who commanded light to shine out of darkness, who has shone in our hearts to give the light of the knowledge of the glory of God in the* face *of Jesus Christ. But we have this treasure in earthen vessels, that the excellence of the power may be of God and not of us.*

Proverbs 13:9: *The light of the righteous rejoices, but the lamp of the wicked will be put out*. Here the Bible clearly identifies how our lives are likened to a lamp. A lamp which, in the case of the wicked, will one day be extinguished. This is the tragic end that far too many people will one day face.

But if the lamp represents the life of each of us, we can take hope that our lamp will be kept burning in the Lord.

Psalm 18:28: *For You will light my lamp; The Lord my God will enlighten my darkness.*

When God first established His dwelling place among His people, the *Mishkan* – or Tabernacle – He designed the Sanctuary to be lit up constantly by a lampstand or *Menorah*. The lampstand had a specific design – a single stem with two sets of identical branches coming off the central stem, from the right and from the left, which we will look at later.

Part of the Priest's daily role was to trim the wicks and top up the oil morning and evening, in order to keep the lamp burning.

Leviticus 24:3 (NLT): *This is the lampstand that stands in the Tabernacle, in front of the inner curtain that shields the Ark of the Covenant. Aaron must keep the lamps burning in the Lord's presence all night. This is a permanent law for you, and it must be observed from* *generation to generation.*

The lampstand was to be kept burning throughout the night, in the presence of the Lord. It was to never be extinguished. Nor was it to be allowed to be quenched. This task has not left the Priesthood, even though we no longer have the physical Tabernacle, or Temple, to visit. We are God's royal priesthood (1 Peter 2:5, 9), and the daily duty of keeping the light burning has been passed on to us, so the Light of the World can continuously shine through us in the night.

How does God "light my lamp"? When we accept Jesus, God lights the Holy Place within His "new Temple"... of which you are (1 Corinthians 3:17; 1 Corinthians 6:19), through His Word:

Psalm 119:105: *Your word is a lamp to my feet and a light to my path.*

And through the way we live according to His laws, His commandments and statutes:

Proverbs 6:23: *For the commandment is a lamp, And the law a light; Reproofs of instruction are the way of life.*

1 John 1:5-7: *This is the message which we have heard from Him and declare to you, that God is light and in Him is no darkness at all. If we say that we have fellowship with Him, and walk in darkness, we lie and do not practice the truth. But if we walk in the light as He is in the light, we have fellowship with one another, and the blood of Jesus Christ His Son cleanses us from all sin.*

Each of us has been given the same "lamp" to hold and to maintain. How we go about using our lamps differs for all of us. Some of us are wise in the way we look after our lamps; others of us are more foolish. But none of us can help another maintain their lamps, in the same way the wise virgins in Jesus' parable couldn't share their spare oil with their foolish friends. As we await the arrival of the Bridegroom, we each have a responsibility to keep our wicks trimmed.

In a lamp, the wick supplies fuel to the flame by drawing up the oil to be burned. By that same token, in this parable, the wick is the action we take, on a daily basis, to keep the flame alive in our lives. As believers, this action stems from the relationship we have with the Light Himself, the action we take to keep Yeshua alive in us and our relationship with Him burning strong. This is the action of reading and studying His Word, putting into action His commandments, to abide in Him, regularly communicating with Him.

The wick is what ignites the oil. It is the faith we exercise when we step out into the things of God, not knowing what the result will be. It is putting into action Biblical principles as best we can, through the way we live our lives. It is moving, when prompted by the Holy Spirit, into the things of God – whether using the gifts of the Spirit, or offering a cup of water in love. The wick ignites the Light of the World to be seen in and through us, constantly, to the darkness around us. It is faith accompanying works, for without faith, it is impossible to please God (Hebrews 11:6).

But just as a wick is nothing without the oil, so are all our attempts at keeping the flame alight useless without the oil being topped up in us regularly. So what does the oil represent?

The oil represents the Holy Spirit. We are to keep ourselves topped up with Him. But more than that we need to allow ourselves to be soaked in Him. A friend and colleague, Janey, who lived and worked in Jerusalem with her husband for five years, recently told me about the process involved in making the lamps ready for use. The lamps, which are made of clay, have to be soaked in water before the oil can be added. If this doesn't occur, the oil will seep through the clay, and the lamp will be rendered useless. In the same way, as we accept Yeshua, we are soaked in Him. This allows the "oil" of the Holy Spirit to be used through these clay vessels (2 Corinthians 4:7).

Without the anointing of the Holy Spirit we are not any different to those who are in the world; our works are just us trying to make God accept us. We need the Holy Spirit to empower us from the inside, so that like a river, He can flow out through us, causing the Light to shine and affect every place we go.

We, as the Bride of Christ, are called to be ready. And as we see in the parable of the ten virgins, there is a stark warning that if we are not ready, we will miss the wedding – and once the doors are shut, they are shut!

Matthew 25:10-12: *"And while they went to buy, the bridegroom came, and those who were ready went in with him to the wedding;* ***and the door was shut****. Afterward the other virgins came also, saying, 'Lord, Lord, open to us!' But he answered and said, 'Assuredly, I say to you, I do not know you.' "Watch therefore, for you know neither the day nor the hour in which the Son of Man is coming."* (Emphasis is author's own.)

It is all too easy for us to blame others for our problems, but the Bible is clear that each of us is responsible for our own preparation. On an airplane, when the stewards are giving the safety announcement before the flight takes off, parents with young children are reminded, in the case of an emergency, they will need to put on their own safety masks *before* they can put the mask on their children. The reason for this is very simple. How can a mother or a father ensure they meet the needs of their offspring, when they are struggling to breathe themselves, or they collapse from a lack of oxygen?

Our natural instinct is to want to ensure our children are going to be OK, but the only way we can achieve this is to make sure we ourselves are OK first. In the same way, we ourselves need to ensure we are awake and alert, not sleeping, ready to meet the Bridegroom when He arrives. Otherwise we may end up watching in horror as those we love are whisked off to join in the wedding feast, but we are left outside.

Conversely, we want to do what we can to encourage and support others to be ready too, so they don't miss out on meeting Jesus when He returns for His Bride. We can't take the attitude of "I'm going to heaven so I'm alright, Jack". The crowds who were listening to Jesus as He was speaking would have understood from their wedding traditions that, as the cry started to go out, "the bridegroom is coming", their role was to ensure that the message was passed on, from neighbour-to-neighbour, household-to-household, village-to-town, until eventually everyone knew for certain that the bridegroom was on his way.

As participants of the wedding feast, we have to pass the message on – we can't keep it for ourselves! We have to do our bit to ensure the message reaches everyone who needs to know. And who needs to know the message of "Jesus will be returning for His bride"?

Acts 1:8 (NLT): *"…you will be my witnesses, telling people about me everywhere—in Jerusalem, throughout Judea, in Samaria, and to the ends of the earth."*

Again, let's pause for a moment – there's more: when the groom's friends were announcing the arrival of the bridegroom, they would shout, "Look! The bridegroom comes," followed by the blowing of shofars (trumpets), and generally lots of noise! If you are a regular reader

of Scripture, this will sound familiar:
Matthew 24: 30-31: *"…they will see the Son of Man coming on the clouds of heaven with power and great glory. And He will send His angels with a great sound of a trumpet, and they will gather together His elect from the four winds, from one end of heaven to the other."*
1 Thessalonians 4:16: *For the Lord Himself will descend from heaven with a shout, with the voice of an archangel, and with the trumpet of God.*

How awesome it will be when the cries go out – "Look! The Bridegroom is coming!" – as Jesus returns for us! This is another *selah* moment – as all the noise of all the carnivals in the world cannot compare to the joy and excitement of that Great Day!

Chapter Eight

It is Time!

Revelation 19:7: *Let us be glad and rejoice and give Him glory, for the marriage of the Lamb has come, and His wife has made herself ready.*

So now the word has spread, and the bride-to-be is aware her hour has come, when she is to be received by her groom. She needs to gather her attendants, wash, change into her wedding garments, fix her hair and makeup, and go out to receive him. The excitement is strong within her, as her heart pounds with each action she makes, understanding that the waiting period has reached its climax with the imminent arrival of her soon-to-be husband. Her smile grows. Her joy spills over as laughter and giggling fills the air around her, affecting her family and friends gathering with her, until the moment of her departure finally arrives.

Now is the time. Her groom has arrived. She needs to leave her father and mother's household, and be joined to her husband. The final act of preparation for the bride was the addition of her veil, just as Rebekah, the wife of our forefather Isaac, added her veil at the moment before she met with her future husband.

Genesis 24:64-65: *Then Rebekah lifted her eyes, and when she saw Isaac she dismounted from her camel; for she had said to the servant, "Who is this man walking in the field to meet us?" The servant said, "It is my master."*

So she took a veil and covered herself. (Emphasis is author's own.)

The veil symbolised the bride's chastity, modesty, purity, dignity and virtue as a woman and future wife – a woman who has waited for her husband to return, and can walk out to meet him, her head held high, with graceful honour. Her neck strong and proud, beautiful as the tower of David (***Song of Songs 4:4***).

In this simple act, Rebekah was portraying the type of character she was to her future husband. She was demonstrating her modesty, purity and virtue as his future wife.

I find it interesting a veil is called a veil. One of the definitions for the word is: "Something that covers, separates, screens or conceals."[15] The veil was used to cover the face of the bride, in order to separate her from the rest of the wedding party. She was separated as the one for whom the groom was waiting.

In the Old Testament, the veil was another item of fabric used to cover or separate. In the Tabernacle, the heavy curtain which was used to separate the people from God, was called The Veil. It was intended to cover them from looking upon His glory, by accident, for no one could look upon God and live (Exodus 33:20). This was not because He didn't want to be looked at by His people, but because God is so holy, our sin cannot remain in His presence, just as darkness cannot remain in the presence of the light. The sinful nature of our old self causes us to hide from God (as Adam and Eve did as soon as they had sinned). But when we enter into His presence through The Veil – that is through Yeshua (Hebrews 10:20), we can enter in with boldness because Jesus veils us with His righteousness. He covers us. He separates us, that we may enter into the fullness of the relationship God designed us to have with Him!

In the same way, the Veil of Jesus' righteousness covers us, His Bride, indicating that we have been washed in His blood, so we are seen as being cleansed, purified and made virtuous as Yeshua's Bride, clear for all of heaven to see, clear to the Father that His Son's Bride is a good companion for Him to be in a relationship with. We do not stand in our own strength; rather we are seen through the covering of our Husband – of our returning Groom – of our Saviour.

Once the veil had been placed over her, now the bride-to-be was fully dressed. Now she was fully ready. Now she would go out to greet her husband. The bride-to-be would be escorted by her parents, family and attendants to the meeting place of the couple – the *Chuppah* – usually at the groom's father's house. This is where they would now finalise their marriage, at the *nisu'in* ceremony in front of the wedding guests who were already assembled, having heard the shout, as it was passed along, of "the groom is coming".

Under the *Chuppah*, the couple would receive a blessing from the groom's father and share a second cup of wine – the Cup of Rejoicing – as a fully married couple, before a ring was placed on the bride's finger.

The sides of the *Chuppah* would be drawn around the groom and his new wife. There, in that secluded place, they would consummate their marriage-covenant, while their family and friends waited outside.

Once the marriage had been consummated, the groom would emerge from the chamber and proudly announce to all who were gathered that he and his wife were now one in union. John the Baptist alluded to this when he spoke of himself as being the fore-runner to Christ:

John 3:29: *"He who has the bride is the bridegroom;*

but the friend of the bridegroom, who stands and hears him, rejoices greatly because of the bridegroom's voice. Therefore this joy of mine is fulfilled." John expressed his joy and delight at the union of his close friend, the Groom, to His precious Bride.

This now led to the beginning of the final celebrations of the *nisu'in* (*Nisu'in* comes from the Hebrew word *no'say* which means to carry; meaning that the husband was now carrying the burden of the bride, rather than she being carried by her father), whereby the family and friends of the couple would celebrate for the next seven days (sometimes called "the seven days of the *Chuppah*")! Word spread around the community who would also come and join in the festivities, enjoying feasts and banquets and making merry! At the end of the seven days of celebrations, the groom would bring his wife out of the chamber, her veil now removed, and he would proudly present his wife to all his guests!

This is why the guests would have to be ready around the time of the expected return of the groom. As previously mentioned, everyone knew it would be approximately twelve months after the groom had left, before he would come to receive his bride, so after the year was up, there was an air of expectation from all the wedding guests. Most people would begin to prepare themselves as soon as the twelve months was up, so they would not be caught unawares.

Revelation 16:15: *"Behold, I am coming as a thief. Blessed is he who watches, and keeps his garments, lest he walk naked and they see his shame."*

Matthew 22:11-13: *"But when the king came in to see the guests, he saw a man there who did not have on a wedding garment. So he said to him, 'Friend, how did you come in here without a wedding garment?' And* *he was speechless. Then the king said to the servants, 'Bind him hand and foot, take him away, and cast him into outer darkness; there will be weeping and gnashing of teeth.'"*

Could you imagine going to a wedding and one of the guests being dressed inappropriately? Would any of us in our right minds plan to attend a wedding in a tatty pair of jeans and a ripped top? Not at all! As guests of the couple, we make every effort to look good. It's a celebration. Plus we don't want to be reminded of how bad we looked when we get invited to their new home and see the big group wedding picture proudly on display – Oh the shame!

How offended would you be, if one of your guests turned up to your wedding looking as though they couldn't be bothered to make the effort? No matter how gracious you think you might be, you wouldn't want them to appear in your wedding photos, and some of you would do the same thing as the king in Jesus' parable – throw them out!

There's an understood protocol for guests at a wedding, of how we are to dress and behave. When we accept the invitation to attend the wedding, we accept the rules and regulations of the wedding. There are certain expectations laid upon us as we accept the invitation to sit in the Wedding Ceremony and celebrate with the couple at the Reception.

In the same way, there are principles of holiness at the great wedding feast. God has categorically told us through His Word that He has certain expectations of us. There are principles of holiness which He requires of us to allow His Holy Spirit to work in us, so we may be a reflection of Him. When a couple have been married for a long time, they often become a reflection of each other, to the point where an "outsider" can recognise who a husband's wife is.

Everyone had a part to play in the traditional Jewish wedding, and would have known that part of their responsibilities was having their lamps always burning, ready for the glorious street procession; and being appropriately dressed, they would be ready to join in the pageant.

We too need to be ready, whether we *realise* we are actually the Bride of Yeshua, or think we are just to be a guest. Either way, there is no escaping the fact that God expects us to be ready for His Son's arrival to claim His Bride!

Chapter Nine

The Groom of the Old Testament

The idea of Jesus being likened to a Bridegroom, who will soon come to take His Bride home with Him, is not limited to the New Testament. Throughout the Old Testament, we see how the marriage covenant and a relationship between a husband and wife were often used to illustrate the relationship between God and His People, Israel.

Isaiah 54:5: *"For your Maker is your husband, The Lord of hosts is His name; And your Redeemer is the Holy One of Israel; He is called the God of the whole earth."*

Whenever God was angry or saddened by the departure of His people away from Him and His ways, He likened them to an adulterous wife: ***Ezekiel 16:32:*** *"You are an adulterous wife, who takes strangers instead of her husband."*

And when God speaks of the return of His people to Him, in that Day when God shows mercy upon them, He describes it to Hosea as a husband who is attracting His Bride to Him.

Hosea 2:14–20: *"Therefore, behold, I will allure her, will bring her into the wilderness, And speak comfort to her... "And it shall be, in that day," Says the Lord, "That you will call Me 'My Husband,' And no longer call Me 'My Master,' For I will take from her mouth the names of the Baals, And they shall be remembered by* *their name no more. "I will betroth you to Me forever; Yes, I will betroth you to Me In righteousness and justice, In lovingkindness and mercy; I will betroth you to Me in faithfulness, And you shall know the Lord."*

Leviticus 26:40-44 (NLT): *"But at last My people will confess their sins and the sins of their ancestors for betraying Me and being hostile toward Me... Then I will remember My covenant with Jacob and My covenant with Isaac and My covenant with Abraham, and I will remember the land... At last the people will pay for their sins, for they have continually rejected My regulations and despised my decrees. "But despite all this,* ***I will not utterly reject or despise them*** *while they are in exile in the land of their enemies.* ***I will not cancel my covenant with them*** *by wiping them out, for I am the Lord their God."* (Emphasis is author's own).

This relationship was not broken, when Jesus came, bringing with Him the message of hope and reconciliation to all people. It was not broken when the disciples realised the message was to the Jew first, and then to the Gentile. It was not broken as they spread out around the world sharing the gospel of *Yeshua HaMashiach* (Jesus the Messiah). It was not broken thousands of years later as the Church spread among the nations. No! The marriage covenant God made with His people is from everlasting to everlasting. He says in the passage we just read from Hosea, that He has betrothed the children of Israel to Him forever. Forever, by definition, has no end point!

And what a faithful Husband He is, waiting patiently throughout history for His Bride to return her attention to Him!

Chapter Ten

Inside the *Chuppah* – Approaching the Holy Place

As we saw in chapter eight, the bride and groom would be joined together under the *Chuppah*. This was a special place of intimacy hidden away from their guests, where husband and wife could finally be together, alone. After twelve months of separation – this was a valuable moment for them.

But not every Jewish man or woman would enter into a *Chuppah* in their lifetime. Only those who were entering into a covenant marriage relationship; and those who did enter in, would only do so once in their lifetime (in theory) as marriage was to be a lifelong commitment between a man and his wife.

This reminds me of the Priestly duties which involved one priest entering into the Most Holy Place, or The Holy of Holies, once a year – each would have one opportunity in his lifetime to enter into this most intimate of places with the Lord Almighty. It was not a duty the priest took lightly; the preparation and consecration would have been as intense as a bride preparing for her wedding day (Leviticus 16).

He was required to wash himself thoroughly, cleansing himself in the *mikvah* (ritual Temple bath) in between the strictly laid out stages of the numerous sacrifices required for the Day of Atonement (*Yom Kippur*). The High Priest was obliged to change His clothes each time after cleansing himself, wearing specially consecrated, holy, linen garments to enter into the Holy of Holies, where God resided (the only time he wore this outfit, and then it would be discarded after the Priest had performed his duties). In no other fashion could he enter this Most Holy of rooms, and at no other time.

God has always had a desire to live amongst us, to be right in the centre of our daily lives – just as the positioning of the Tabernacle demonstrates, when it was set up *right* in the centre of the Israelites camp (Numbers 2:2). But God was so holy He could not look upon the sin of humanity. No one could enter the presence of God and live. Not because God had it in mind to kill mankind but because evil cannot stand in the presence of God.

Inside the Holy of Holies, the Priest could walk right into the very presence of God; an honour the average human being would never experience. But God wanted to have a more personable relationship with His people. He wanted to provide a way for us to enter into His presence – freely, and more regularly. He wanted us to draw near to Him, and to enjoy intimate moments with Him, where He would talk with us and where He would listen to our petitions and conversations with Him, as often as we would approach Him.

In the *Chuppah*, a bride and groom would begin a dialogue which was to last the duration of their relationship (remember they had not spoken to each other during the time of their separation) – entering into this intimate place would involve conversation, listening and talking, as husband and wife would begin the lifetime "job" of knowing one another.

The Bible often describes a union between a man and woman by the phrase, "And … *knew his wife*" (eg: Adam, Genesis 4:1). I believe this time of "knowing each other" would involve more than the mere sexual union between a couple. I believe it was to become a place of rest, where the intimacy of a husband "knowing" his wife extended to the intimate conversation between a husband and wife; the feeling of a warm embrace, which allowed both parties to feel safe and secure in the relationship. I believe there would follow a discussion of plans, dreams, hopes and aspirations for the future, as the husband lay in the arms of his wife (reference, Samson and Delilah – see Judges 16).

God doesn't need to feel "safe and secure" by His relationship with us, but in inviting us to enter into His presence, He is providing us with an opportunity to feel safe and secure against the world. So that when we emerge from our time with Him, we can stand in His strength against all the enemy throws our way. This can only come through our regularly entering into the place of intimacy with Him, where He will renew us, cause us to rise with *"wings like eagles, They shall run and not be weary, They shall walk and not faint"* (***Isaiah 40:31***) and where He will share His dreams and plans – if we will take the time to listen to Him (Amos 3:7).

But just as a priest didn't enter into the Holy of Holies for his own benefit – he was acting on behalf of the people in his approaching God – so we too should be approaching God for the benefit of those who are not yet in a position to approach Him for themselves. The priest would seek retribution – or atonement – for the people of Israel. He would ask God to forgive them for their wrong doings, and to cleanse them of their unrighteousness so they could remain written in His book of life and not be scrubbed out. According to Jewish tradition, God writes the destiny of His people into a book for the year ahead, the Book of Life. Ten days later, on *Yom Kippur*, He "seals" His verdict based on the sacrifices and atonement made on their behalf.

But as we read in Hebrews 9 and 10, Jesus fulfilled this need for the blood sacrifice atonement once and for all when He died upon the cross. The Veil in the Temple, separating God from His people was torn – by God Himself (Matthew 27:51) – as a demonstration of the access into the "*Chuppah*" which was now made possible. No longer does God judge us on a yearly basis – He lives among us and keeps us on His path daily. No longer is it down to one Priest to enter into the presence of God on behalf of the people, Jesus, the Great High Priest (see for example Hebrews 3 - 4) made it possible for everyone to enter in.

How wonderful it is to know we now have the freedom, through the blood of Yeshua, to enter into the Holy of holies – or the *Chuppah* – as much as we want, and rest awhile with our Heavenly Groom. How amazing it is to understand that Creator God desires to "know you" intimately, so He can reveal the depth of His heart to you. How awesome to know that He delights in us and wants to know us, but more than that – He wants us to be open and real with Him. To lay aside our masks when we come before Him and openly admit when we mess up. Then He can forgive us our sins and cleanse us from all unrighteousness (1 John 1:9), preparing us for the Day when He can present us cleansed and pure to His Son (2 Corinthians 4:14). He wants to strengthen us for the battles ahead, and pass on to us the strategies He has already drawn up for a successful fight. As a wife is a helpmate to her husband (Genesis 2:18), so we are to be a helper to the Lord in these last days.

And just as a woman has boldness to draw close to her husband when they are married, we also have boldness to draw close to our Groom. We don't need to be afraid. We don't need to hang about at the entrance.

I remember taking a group of young people to a Youth Conference organised by "Serious For God" (The Youth branch for Elim). This was a group of young people from the East of London, who were most comfortable expressing themselves and their love for God through Rap, Gospel and Soul. Taking them to the national gathering, they were suddenly faced with a completely different style of worship they were not used to, as the Worship Team mainly rock. Most of them stood at the back of the venue, arms folded watching what was happening around them. I felt so sad for them because they had brought the East End attitude with them up to the Midlands, and were not able to engage in the "new" style of music. As I prayed for them, the Lord showed me how this group represented many in the Church who have pre-conceived ideas of what they think they can draw near to God with. But in reality, all they are doing is hanging around in the outer courts, not able to engage with the Lord, and keeping a distance from the Holy Place – and especially from the Holy of Holies. They watch what is happening, through the windows of opportunity, never actually stepping in themselves. I am happy to say the Holy Spirit moved amongst this group, and most of the young people let go of their pre-conceived ideas to meet with God in that place. What about you? Are you on the outside looking in, or are you inside – right in the presence of your Bridegroom?

We don't need to wait for a "royal invitation" (as Esther was required to do when she wanted to approach the king [Esther 4:11]). We can approach our Groom with confidence. Hallelujah!

Chapter Eleven

Being Ready

Part of our preparation process is to ensure we know *exactly* where we are going. It is important for us to have an understanding of where the wedding will be taking place and how we are to get there. I remember hearing about a friend of a couple who were getting married. The friend thought he knew where he was going, so he didn't bother to check the route with a route planner before setting off. The truth was, the Church he had in his mind, where the ceremony was taking place, was the wrong Church! He almost ended up at the wedding of a total stranger!

As believers, we have a confidence in the Holy Spirit as our guarantee of where we are going. But the Bible also gives us clear guidelines as to *how* we are to get there. Jesus often spoke about the end of time, and the Day of Judgement. He gave us guidelines we should follow in order to arrive at our destination. A read through the four Gospels in the New Testament will tell us in Jesus' own words, without even looking at the rest of the Scriptures!

For example, studying the Beatitudes in Matthew 5 to 7 shows how even in this small section, Jesus provides us with clear instructions on how we are to live. The foundational premise Jesus taught is love. Love of the Father with all our heart, all our soul and all our mind, and to love others as ourselves (Matthew 22:37-40). How amazing would it have been to have sat on the mountain listening as Jesus taught a fresh way of putting into action the Scriptures – not to do away with the old laws, but rather simplifying them. Some of the laws which we have allowed to seep into our churches and lives today are not so dissimilar to the religious bondages that the religious leaders had placed upon the people when Jesus lived. We seem to have forgotten the fact that we have freely received, so we should freely give (Matthew 10:8). But imagine how it would be if we were to put into action this type of love – the world couldn't help but notice Yeshua alive in us, and be drawn to Him.

Empty religion can include anything which is an "added extra" to the Bible, anything which we try to add to God's instructions or His Word, in order to enhance what we believe God expects of us. This is often where our judgement of others comes in. (See Matthew 7 – Do *not* judge....) The religious authorities in the time of Jesus were guilty of *hypocritical* judgement, and we have to be aware of that danger in ourselves.

At the end of the day, Jesus left not only the guidelines for us verbally, He Himself is the example we are called to follow. He proved to us that it *is* achievable for us to live in the way He describes. Of course, we know He is perfect, and we are not, but this should not be a cop-out clause for us to not even try. If we abide in Christ, He will abide in us and His Holy Spirit will help us. That's how it is being in relationship with Yeshua.

1 John 2:3-6: *Now by this we know that we know Him, if we keep His commandments. He who says, "I know Him," and does not keep His commandments, is a liar, and the truth is not in him. But whoever keeps His word, truly the love of God is perfected in him. By this we know that we are in Him. He who says he abides in Him ought* *himself also to walk just as He walked.*

Jesus expects it of us to at least attempt to work out our salvation in Him – not to take for granted His sacrifice for us, without living out His Word and example in this life, lest by our constant sinning, we condemn Yeshua to be sacrificed over and over (Hebrews 9:26-28).

Hebrews 9:28: *"But so Christ was* ***offered once to bear the sins of many. To those who eagerly wait for Him He will appear a second time****, apart from sin, for salvation."* (Emphasis is author's own).

Part of our preparation also has to involve looking at the areas of our lives where we know we will be judged by God on that Great Day. We can spend all our time dreaming and thinking about the Great Wedding of the Bridegroom to His Bride, but part of our preparation process is a purification process. We are called to be holy, just as He is holy. A bride-to-be will spend time cleansing her behaviour, as we have already discussed. So in our getting ready for the Great Day of the Lord, we need to really hold the mirror of God's Word up to our hearts and take a long, hard look at ourselves through it.

There are at least three areas the Bible says we, as followers of Yeshua, will be judged:

1. In accordance with the words we speak, ***Matthew 12:36-37:*** *"But I say to you that for every idle word men may speak,* ***they will give account of it in the Day of Judgment****. For by your words you will be justified, and by your words you will be condemned."* This includes denying Jesus, or being embarrassed by Him. If we deny Jesus, He will deny us before the Father (Matthew 10:33).

2. In accordance with the way we live out the calling and purposes of God in our lives, ***2 Corinthians 5:10:***

For we must all appear before the judgment seat of Christ, that each one may receive the things done in the body*, according to what he has done, whether good or bad.* And ***1 Corinthians 3:11-15:*** *For no other foundation can anyone lay than that which is laid, which is Jesus Christ. Now if anyone builds on this foundation with gold, silver, precious stones, wood, hay, straw,* ***each one's work will become clear****; for the Day will declare it, because it will be revealed by fire; and* ***the fire will test each one's work, of what sort it is****. If anyone's work which he has built on it endures, he will receive a reward. If anyone's work is burned, he will suffer loss; but he himself will be saved, yet so as through fire.* (Emphasis is author's own.)

3. In accordance with the standards we uphold and by which we judge others, ***Matthew 7:1-2:*** *"Judge not, that you be not judged. For with what judgment you judge,* ***you will be judged****; and with the measure you use, it will be measured back to you."*

This tells me how seriously God's Word should be taken, and the awareness that we, as the Bride of Jesus, need in relation to how we are living this life. Not that we can get to heaven by works, because we cannot. We get to heaven through Jesus Christ – and Him alone! But the rewards we receive, the place reserved for us in heaven, how close we are to the throne of God, these are tied up in how we live life here. Sure – you could make a commitment to accept Jesus Christ as your Lord and Saviour – good for you! But living a life sold-out for God, worthy of bearing His name has a different connotation. Even in Jesus' letter to the Churches of Asia in Revelation, Jesus talks of the rewards He has laid up for those who endure to the end, including the special place under the altar for those who are martyred for His name. Even the disciples understood there was a position to be gained as they argued between themselves who would be seated at Jesus' right hand, which was the place of highest honour in Jewish tradition (Mark 9:33-37; Matthew 20:20-28).

If I look back over my own life, I know there are times I have messed up. I have taught one thing in Bible Study, but then gone and done the opposite of what I had taught. I have been asked to do something, and done it, but in my heart I have grumbled. I have judged people according to how I think they should live, only to fall short of my own standards. All of these are things I know the Lord will pull me up on, one embarrassing, unpleasant, unholy, ungodly situation by one. I can't argue against Him, because I know I am guilty. The enemy will try to expose me even more, condemning me and criticising me, but *Jesus* is my Saviour and in Him I know I can have full access to the presence of God. Not just in my life on this earth – but in heaven too! I know there are those things which I have done which, when tested by the fire of God, will be burned up and turned to ashes – because they are worthless at the end of the day. But I also know that the Holy Spirit has led me on many occasions to get it right! These things, these works I have built up for the kingdom of God will be refined through the fire and gleam as gold, silver and precious stones – forever to glorify my Father in Heaven! Hallelujah!

What about you, friend? If you were to look at all the things you have done – in the name of the Lord, or even without being aware of Who you were serving, how much of it will survive the fire of God on that Great Day? I believe we will all say, "But Lord when did I do that"

When He praises us for the kindness we demonstrated to others (Matthew 25:35-40). Sadly, in the same vein, there will also be people in the Church who will say, "But Lord, didn't I do this and that for you" (Matthew 7:21:23), but they will realise – too late – they weren't known by the Lord. We can't get into heaven by works alone. Works in themselves are meaningless to God. Many religions pride themselves on their works. It is only through a relationship with the Bridegroom – Jesus – that we have access to God in Heaven.

Please don't think on that Great Day, God's only intention will be to shame you – oh no! That is *not* what He is about. He is holy, He is pure – He can *only* allow the holiest and purest in His Kingdom. Remember the Garden of Eden? Adam and Eve were not expelled because God was ashamed of them. No – He was heartbroken, because He knew the purest relationship He had with His creation was now marred, and would not be restored until the chosen time in the future – through the sacrifice His Precious Son Jesus was to pay on our behalf! They were expelled because they were no longer holy, as sin had crept into their hearts and minds and souls.

The laws and sacrifices laid out by God to Moses were a way for mankind to be made holy, to be purified and cleansed – through the shedding of blood, but God knew a day would be coming when only the purest blood of a Holy Man would be the ultimate way for us to be made right with Him.

As we prepare for His return, God is in the process – through the Holy Spirit – of purifying and restoring holiness to His Church. So that when He gathers us up on that Great Day, for our final purifying in His refining fire, He can present to the Bridegroom – His Son – a Bride who is pure, blemish-free and holy. Oh how glorious a sight she will be on that Day!

But the Bride of Christ is not weak and pathetic – *no*! She is a reflection of her Betrothed. She is virtuous, strong and mighty – a force to be reckoned with! She is persistent, determined and faithful. Just as a wife is a reflection of her husband, the Bride of Christ is a reflection of Him to the world, to those who do not know Him. Through the love she demonstrates, the world will see the love of Jesus for His Bride. They will see the love of God for themselves!

Chapter Twelve

The Warrior Bride[16]

I remember having a vivid dream in 2006. This was a dream I understood to be about the Church and our need to "be ready"! In this dream, I saw a group of people, mostly friends of mine at the time, who represented the Church, living, working, playing on a large green. Everyone was busy "doing life", washing, cleaning, playing games together. There was a stream running at the side of the green, and as I walked up through the groups of people, the stream became a river at the top of the green. Across the river on the other side was a large gathering of what looked like toy soldiers – some on horses, some on elephants, all holding weapons.

The toy soldiers started to march towards the river bank on their side and I realised they were an advancing army. I ran through the people on my side of the river shouting, "The enemy is advancing, come on we need to get ready to fight!" But no one was moving.

"*Come on!* We need to take up our positions – the enemy is coming!" People looked over the river and saw the toy soldiers. They started to laugh. "They're not a threat to us – they're only toys." Everyone carried on doing what they were doing.

The dream cut to another scene – still on the green. Again people were playing games. I was washing something in the stream to the right of the green and suddenly heard something. I looked to my left and saw in the distance a dust cloud. I stood up and realised that our armies were physically being pushed back by the advancing enemy. They were no longer toy soldiers. They were huge. Creatures on elephants were pushing the army of the Lord of Hosts back. I ran towards them shouting as I went trying to stir people to join me to try and help our armies fight against the advancing enemy.

This dream is as vivid to me today as it was back in 2006.

When God led the people of Israel out of the Land of Egypt, they had become enslaved to the Egyptian people – slaves of a powerful nation – slaves who were trampled on and treated harshly. You might expect them to have a bit of a victim mentality, with having been downtrodden for 430 years, as generation to generation, the people of Israel stopped being friends of Egypt – under the leading of Pharaoh's right-hand man Joseph, and became slaves, "afflicted" by harsh "taskmasters" who were "in dread of the children of Israel" (Exodus chapter 1 tells the story!). But they did not leave as a people who were burdened or a victim of cruel circumstances. They left victorious. They left strong. They left together, as one people. They left as an army. ***Exodus 13:18b (NLT):*** *Thus the Israelites left Egypt* ***like an army ready for battle*** (Emphasis is author's own). The people God led out of Egypt were "like an army ready for battle"! The Jewish text states that the Israelites were fully armed! This is the people of God!

Anyone who has studied, or understands the nature of God, will know He is the Lord of Hosts (see for reference Psalm 24:10; Psalm 46; Psalm 59:5; Isaiah 28; the book of Zechariah). The Hebrew word for the "Lord of Hosts" is "*Jehovah Sabaoth*" which literally means "Lord of Hosts of Armies". God is a Mighty Warrior. God is our

Great Deliverer. He fights the battle on behalf of His people (2 Chronicles 20:15). Whoever touches God's people may as well be touching the very apple of His eye (Zechariah 2:8), and as we have already discussed, He is like a jealous husband. I would not want to poke *Jehovah Sabaoth* in the eye, for the reaction He will give!

This is all well and good for the people of Israel of the Scriptures, you may be thinking, but how does that relate to the Bride of Yeshua today? Jesus is God, therefore one of His titles is *Jehovah Sabaoth*. And Messianic thought states that the "Commander of God's Army" Joshua meets with in Joshua 5:13-15, is a pre-incarnational meeting with Jesus – a Theophany. Therefore as Jesus is the Commander of God's army, as His followers, we are His soldiers. Paul urges Timothy to be mindful of Who he is serving, and the endurance which is required from him as he serves his Captain:

2 Timothy 2:3-4: *You therefore must endure hardship as a good soldier of Jesus Christ. No one engaged in warfare entangles himself with the affairs of this life, that he may please him who enlisted him as a soldier.*

The Bride of Jesus has been enlisted as His army. We are engaged in a spiritual battle (Ephesians 6:12). We have been given "weapons of warfare" which are "mighty for the pulling down of strongholds" (2 Corinthians 10:4), such as the "Sword of the Spirit" (Ephesians 6:17). And we have been given a protective Armour to wear for the battle (Ephesians 6:13-18), including the "Breastplate of Righteousness", "Helmet of Salvation" and the "Shield of Faith". We are the Bride of Yeshua, but we are also part of His army. We are the Warrior Bride!

Joel 2:11 says that *The Lord gives voice before His army, For His camp is very great....* I believe God is trying to warn His army, His Warrior Bride, that the enemy is not as weak as we have made him out to be.

Too many of us are playing at Church. Too many of us are busy doing life. Too many of us will not be ready when the Lord returns to fight satan once and for all. Too many of us are in danger of being left behind.

I don't believe Jesus is being defeated – not in the slightest. He is *victorious!* When He died and rose again, He ultimately beat satan and holds the keys to the gates of hell. I believe Jesus – the Captain of the Lord's Army – is calling His Warrior Bride to action, instead of passivity. Look around you – see what is really going on. Prepare yourself to stand with the Bridegroom. He wants His Warrior Bride by His side. Are you ready for action? Or are you so busy doing your life you haven't noticed the advancement of the kingdom of darkness? Or do you under-estimate the size of the enemy, ridiculing the control he has over the world? Warrior Bride – stand and be strong, for the Day of your Lord is close. Where will *you* be when the roll call is given?

Hebrews 10:22-23: *Let us draw near with a true heart in full assurance of faith, having our hearts sprinkled from an evil conscience and our bodies washed with pure water. Let us* ***hold fast the confession of our hope without wavering****, for He who promised is faithful.* (Emphasis is author's own).

Chapter Thirteen

So Who is Jesus' Bride?

Revelation 21:2 (AMP): *And I saw the holy city, the new Jerusalem, descending out of heaven from God, all arrayed like a bride beautified and adorned for her husband.*

Revelation 21:11 (AMP): *Clothed in God's glory [in all its splendour and radiance]. The lustre of it resembled a rare and most precious jewel, like jasper, shining clear as crystal.*

The Bride of Christ is made up of those who have been brought near through the blood of the Lamb, made alive in Christ. Those who are made one in Him: *one* body; *one* People; *one* Bride; Jewish believer in Yeshua and Gentile believer in Yeshua — two halves made whole in Yeshua Himself who ... *is our peace, who has made both one, and has broken down the middle wall of separation... so as to create in Himself one new man from the two, thus making peace, and that He might reconcile them both to God in one body through the cross....* (See Ephesians 2:14-16). The wall of division has been pulled down between us, just as in 1989, the Berlin Wall was pulled down – which had symbolised the division between the communist bloc and the West; so we can stand as one before Him, stand as one who has been made holy and pure, by the same blood of Jesus, made righteous in Him, as we are presented to Him, at the throne of God – just as a bride, on her wedding day, is presented to her husband, at the altar, before God.

We will stand before the altar of God on that Great Day, one in Christ. This reminds me of something which God told Moses to make according to His design as part of the Tabernacle: the Lampstand which was placed in the Sanctuary or the Holy Place of the Tabernacle. The Tabernacle (*Mishkan*) means "Residence" or "Dwelling place"[17] and it was designed by God to be a physical representation of His dwelling among His people, the Israelites, once they had left Egypt and were headed toward the Promised Land. The Tabernacle was eventually replaced by a more permanent dwelling place for God, by King Solomon, who used designs similar to those given by God to Moses and to His father King David (2 Samuel 7; 1 Chronicles 22; 1 Kings 5-6). The Temple was a grand design, which provided a permanent place for God to live among the Jewish People – until the time of Ezekiel's vision when he saw God leave the Temple (Ezekiel 10).

Both the temporary Tabernacle and the permanent Temple were internally the same design, containing the Sanctuary, or Holy Place, and the Holy of Holies, or Most Holy Place. It was in the Most Holy Place where God dwelt. There were strict rules of how to enter into this part of the building – once a year! In the Holy Place though, the priests were to enter on a daily basis – and it was here where we find the Lampstand. It provided light, in an otherwise darkened room, to the priests as they went about their daily business, and it shone upon the two other items in the room – the Table of Showbread (representing God's divine protection and provision [Exodus 25:23-30]), and the Altar of Incense, (representing the prayers of the priests for the people, [Exodus 30:1-10; Leviticus]).

The Lampstand design was given in ***Exodus 25:31-37 (NLT):*** *Make a lampstand of pure, hammered gold. Make the entire lampstand and its decorations of one piece—the base, centre stem, lamp cups, buds, and petals. Make it with six branches going out from the centre stem, three on each side. Each of the six branches will have three lamp cups shaped like almond blossoms, complete with buds and petals. Craft the centre stem of the lampstand with four lamp cups shaped like almond blossoms, complete with buds and petals. There will also be an almond bud beneath each pair of branches where the six branches extend from the centre stem. The almond buds and branches must all be of one piece with the centre stem, and they must be hammered from pure gold. Then make the seven lamps for the lampstand, and set them so they reflect their light forward.*

So the Lampstand was to have a central shaft coming out from the base, and from that central shaft were to be two sets of identical branches. One set of branches on the left and one set of branches on the right.

The way I see it Jesus is the centre shaft – He called Himself the Light of the World (John 8:12; John 9:5). When we accept Yeshua as Messiah or Jesus as the Christ – whichever language you are most comfortable using – we represent His light in the darkness (the world). He tells us in ***Matthew 5:14:*** *"You are the light of the world. A city that is set on a hill cannot be hidden."* It is through allowing the light of Jesus to shine in and through us, that those around us can see and glorify God (Matthew 5:16. See also Philippians 2:15 and 1 John 1:5-7). When the Light shines, it dispels the darkness and illuminates

Yeshua as the way to forgiveness of sins and an eternal inheritance (Acts 26:18), which is ultimately what we, as the Bride of Christ, are trying to do.

But more than that – the items in the Tabernacle were a physical copy of a spiritual reality (Hebrews 9-10), given specifically to the Jewish People. When John received the Revelation, he had the honour of seeing Jesus, ***Revelation 1:13:*** *". . . in the midst of the seven lampstands One like the Son of Man . . ."* The seven Golden Lampstands represent the seven Churches to whom Jesus was about to address the seven letters He was sending (Revelation 2 and 3).

The Old Testament Tabernacle was a physical representation of God's Heavenly dwelling place. In the New Testament we see the lampstands representing the Church. In Jesus, we see the fulfilment of the Old Covenant, as those who accept Yeshua, the Messiah, as the Son of God are drawn into Him. Jew and Gentile together — two sets of branches held by the same central shaft, Jesus! The Bride of Christ brought together in Him – one new man… a physical copy of what is in heaven. And yet to be seen by us – one new man reconciled in Jesus Himself.

Ephesians 2:14–16: *For He Himself is our peace, who has made both one, and has broken down the middle wall of separation, having abolished in His flesh the enmity, that is, the law of commandments contained in ordinances, so as to create in Himself one new man from the two, thus making peace, and that He might reconcile them both to God in one body through the cross, thereby putting to death the enmity.*

When we read through the Bible we see how God reminds us of the reconciliation we have in Him, reconciliation to Him, and reconciliation to one another.

The Old Covenant wasn't replaced by the life, death and resurrection of Jesus. The Old Covenant was fulfilled in Christ who offered in His flesh the New Covenant of a more personal, personable relationship with the God of the Old Testament. The God of the Jewish People became the God of all people. The special place the Jewish People held in God was opened up to include the Gentiles – through the Veil – that is through Jesus.

Jesus reminds us that He was not planning to replace the Jewish People in the affections of God when He spoke with the woman from Samaria at the well in ***John 4:22:*** *"You worship what you do not know; we know what we worship, for* ***salvation is of the Jews****."* (Emphasis is author's own.) Paul expounded on what Jesus was saying in the opening of his letter to the Church in Rome. ***Romans 1:16:*** *For I am not ashamed of the gospel of Christ, for it is the power of God to salvation for everyone who believes,* ***for the Jew first*** *and also for the Greek.* (Emphasis is author's own.)

This doesn't mean that Jews and Gentiles are segregated. On the contrary, through Yeshua, the Messianic Jewish People (who have accepted Him as their promised Messiah) alongside Gentile Christians, are made as one through our mutual faith in Him. Made one in His body. We are *one people*, serving *one Lord* in *one faith* through *one baptism* – that is baptism of the Holy Spirit. We have been reconciled as *one new man*, through Christ, to become *one people*, a holy priesthood who are brought near to God (Ephesians 2:15).

Jesus describes Himself as a vine and those who abide in Him are the branches. We are His branches, and we are to bear fruit so that through us the Father may be glorified. As we abide in Him, we are joined to who He is and to all the power and authority within Him as He empowers us. Just as a plant draws up nutrients from the soil and "passes it through" the branches to the fruit which is growing.

John 15:1-6: *"I am the true vine, and My Father is the vinedresser. Every branch in Me that does not bear fruit He takes away; and every branch that bears fruit He prunes, that it may bear more fruit. You are already clean because of the word which I have spoken to you. Abide in Me, and I in you. As the branch cannot bear fruit of itself, unless it abides in the vine, neither can you, unless you abide in Me.*

"I am the vine, you are the branches. He who abides in Me, and I in him, bears much fruit; for without Me you can do nothing. If anyone does not abide in Me, he is cast out as a branch and is withered; and they gather them and throw them into the fire, and they are burned."

Jesus knew His listeners would understand what He was saying, as Israel had a long-standing relationship with cultivating vineyards, right from Noah, who was a "farmer and planted a vineyard" (Genesis 9:20). Even as Moses received the Law from God, there were specific mentions of not gleaning from your own vineyard, leaving them for the poor (Leviticus 19:10), or how to pay back another man should your donkey ruin their vineyard (Exodus 22:5)!

But also, the Children of Israel were likened to a vineyard with God as their owner and vinedresser: ***Psalm 80:8:*** *"You have brought a* ***vine*** *out of Egypt; You have cast out the nations, and planted it"*, and ***Isaiah 5:1-7:*** ... *(v.7) "For the vineyard of the Lord of hosts is the house of Israel, And the men of Judah are His pleasant plant."*

What you may not know about vines is that they need to be supported. If we look at the actual growth system of a vine, we see that they rely on "rock exposures, other plants, or other supports for growth, rather than investing energy in a lot of supportive tissue, enabling the plant to reach sunlight with a minimum investment of energy."[18]

What I see here is that Jesus is telling us, that in order to grow, we need to be supported by Him. We could try to "grow" our own way, but without that external support we find in Him, we will be as small as a shrub which doesn't have the support it needs in order to grow as high as it can. The higher a vine can grow the more branches it produces, and fruit it will yield. A vine will expend its energy into yielding fruit, finding the support it needs as it leans on other things: Lean on Yeshua... He will give you rest and support... "...for my burden is light" (Matthew 11:28-30).

So it stands to reason that if there is one Lord, there is only one Vine of which we become a part... one root system which supports and empowers us to bear fruit. Jesus is the source of all we need as we abide in Him. He is the source for *all* those who believe in Him, who abide in Him, each man bearing fruit, each bringing glory to the Father as one whole.

Branches which don't bear fruit in a garden are cut off in order to allow a plant to divert all the nutrients to the branches which are fruitful. When this doesn't happen, the fruit-bearing plants may have some fruit growing, but the fruit is weaker, or not as big or tasty as it could be. So it is necessary for gardeners to prune plants and crops.

Do you see where I am going with this? If not – maybe the Apostle Paul can shed some light on it for you:
Romans 11:16-24: *For if the firstfruit is holy, the lump is also holy; and if the root is holy, so are the branches. And if some of the branches were broken off, and you, being a wild olive tree, were grafted in among*

them, and with them became a partaker of the root and fatness of the olive tree, do not boast against the branches. But if you do boast, remember that you do not support the root, but the root supports you. You will say then, "Branches were broken off that I might be grafted in." Well said. Because of unbelief they were broken off, and you stand by faith. Do not be haughty, but fear. For if God did not spare the natural branches, He may not spare you either. Therefore consider the goodness and severity of God: on those who fell, severity; but toward you, goodness, if you continue in His goodness. Otherwise you also will be cut off. And they also, if they do not continue in unbelief, will be grafted in, for God is able to graft them in again. For if you were cut out of the olive tree which is wild by nature, and were grafted contrary to nature into a cultivated olive tree, how much more will these, who are natural branches, be grafted into their own olive tree?

The olive tree is a very hardy plant. It is drought-, disease- and fire-resistant with a sturdy and extensive root system which is so robust, it is capable of regenerating the tree, even if the plant above-ground is destroyed.[19]

In Greece, grafting the cultivated tree on the wild tree was common practice.[20] We know from Luke's account in Acts, that Paul visited various parts of Greece, e.g. Thessalonika (Acts 17), Athens (Acts 17) and Corinth (Acts 18), so on his travels he would have seen and heard about the practice of grafting in for himself, even if it was not something which was done in Israel at the time. I can imagine Paul walking past an olive garden enquiring about why the olive trees looked different from those in his beloved Israel, and soaking up the information from a local grower, as he listened to the intricate details of how to graft a wild and cultivated tree together.

> "Grafting is a horticultural technique where tissues from one plant are inserted into those of another so the two sets of vascular tissues may join together. This vascular joining is called inosculation. The technique is most commonly used in asexual propagation of commercially grown plants for the horticultural and agricultural trades.
>
> In most cases, one plant is selected for its roots and this is called the stock or rootstock. The other plant is selected for its stems, leaves, flowers, or fruits and is called the scion.
>
> For successful grafting to take place, the vascular cambium (a layer of cells which run through the stem of a plant that is undergoing secondary growth) tissues of the stock and scion plants must be placed in contact with each other. Both tissues must be kept alive until the graft has 'taken', usually a period of a few weeks. Successful grafting only requires that a vascular connection take place between the grafted tissues. Joints formed by grafting are not as strong as naturally formed joints, so a physical weak point often still occurs at the graft, because only the newly formed tissues inosculate (unite or merge) with each other."[21]

It was this lesson in "grafting" which provided Paul with the insight into how God's people and new believers in Yeshua were to work together in the Kingdom of God. Not that the Gentiles were to become Jewish once they had accepted Jesus, nor that Jewish people were to deny their Jewishness and become as the Gentiles when they accepted Yeshua as their prophesied Messiah. No! In Jesus there was a new partnership formed, allowing the two to become merged or joined together, as the root system of the one was meant to provide what was necessary for the new to bear fruit, for the glory of God. The old united with the new in a declaration of the purposes of God for mankind. As all people of all nations became one with the New Covenant – the one new man fully reconciled as the Bride of Yeshua.

What a beautiful picture! The love of God extended throughout history, drawing all men unto Himself, culminating in the presentation of a Bride who has been made whole in Him.

Chapter Fourteen

Declining the Invitation

The highest honour for guests of the bride and groom is reserved for those who are asked to be involved in the wedding party. Many a girl has shared a promise or a pact with her friend about how she will be the chief bridesmaid at her wedding if she gets married first. And the job of the Best Man goes to the one who knows the groom the best – usually the one who knows the worst stories about him!

For the happy couple, choosing the wedding party is not a task to take lightly. Not everyone who wants to be involved can be, and yet there are some friends or siblings who *expect* to be in that elite group for the day. The old Jewish customs for a wedding stipulated it was very insulting for any guest to reject an offer to attend the greatest day of the wedding couple. Even if the role they were offered was not the one they had hoped for.

Luke 14:8–11: *"When you are invited to a wedding feast, don't sit in the seat of honour. What if someone who is more distinguished than you has also been invited? The host will come and say, 'Give this person your seat.' Then you will be embarrassed, and you will have to take whatever seat is left at the foot of the table!*

"Instead, take the lowest place at the foot of the table. Then when your host sees you, he will come and say, 'Friend, we have a better place for you!' Then you will

be honoured in front of all the other guests. For those who exalt themselves will be humbled, and those who humble themselves will be exalted."

How embarrassing to have thought you were invited to a wedding thinking you were an honoured guest, only to be humbled by the bride and groom as you are asked to "make way" for someone who is more revered than you are. In God's Kingdom, the first shall be last and the last shall be first (Mark 9:35); the greatest shall become like the least and the least as the greatest (Matthew 23:11); the leader shall be as the servant and he who serves as one who leads (Luke 22:26).

We can become so full of our own self-importance that not only have we persuaded others of how important we are, convincing ourselves along the way, but we like to think we have God convinced too! How foolish! Jesus came to serve, not to be served. The example He gave for us to follow was to serve those around us. Not so that we can jostle for the "I'm best at being servant-hearted" prize, nor so we can walk around in mock humility – "look at how least I am" – but so we can genuinely lift others above ourselves, in love and compassion, not out of selfish ambition and pride, but looking out for the interests of others (Philippians 2:3-4).

Sure, our minds should always be set on the things of God's kingdom, not on the things of this world (Colossians 3:1-2), but not where we, as Jesus' disciples before us, push and shove for a good position, at the right hand of Jesus, in heaven. For it is better to be invited to the wedding feast, than to not be invited at all!

Luke 14:15(NLT): *Hearing this, a man sitting at the table with Jesus exclaimed, "What a blessing it will be to attend a banquet in the Kingdom of God!"*

But in response to him, Jesus told the parable of the

wedding feast the king was preparing in honour of his son; the impersonal excuses given to the king's son showed how little they thought of their so-called friend. Jesus' Jewish listeners would have felt the full horror of the insult in a way modern readers do not realise. They would have understood Jesus was explaining for whom the wedding feast was reserved.

If you are going to decline the ultimate invitation to the greatest wedding you could ever have the pleasure of attending, you need to make sure you know exactly what you are saying. No excuse, no hindrance, no change of heart will really stand up before God. You can't blame anyone, you can't hide behind anyone, you can't wish you had more time. When the time comes, and you have decided to insult the Father, you need to be sure you can stand on your reasoning. Be sure you know what it is you are rejecting. Understand who it is you will need to give your RSVP card back to, and how you will face Him when you see Him after you have given your rejection.

I can assure you of this one truth. Nothing you think you can offer as a good enough reason for saying "No, thank you" will actually stand up before God. You haven't only rejected His invitation to attend the wedding of His Son Jesus Christ, you have rejected His invitation as the Bride of Christ. You have rejected His offer of love, forgiveness, the removal of your sins, but more importantly, you are rejecting His offer to spend eternity with Him.

Oh be sure friend, tomorrow may seem a long time away, eternity may feel as though it will never come. But when you are separated from God, watching the wedding celebration and not being able to be a part of the festivities, when you are dying for a refreshing, cooling drink on your tongue, or the delicious food laid out on God's table, remember that today was the day you decided to reject His invitation.

Chapter Fifteen

Ready or Not?

Hide and Seek is not a new game, in fact, it is a game which was first played in the Garden of Eden by Adam and Eve, in ***Genesis 3:8:*** *Then the man and his wife heard the sound of the LORD God as he was walking in the garden in the cool of the day, and they hid from the LORD God among the trees of the garden.*

And we've been trying to play the game ever since!

David clearly reminds us there is no way we can hide from God – wherever we go, He is there with us:

Psalm 139:7-12: *Where can I go from Your Spirit? Where can I flee from Your presence? If I go up to the heavens, You are there; if I make my bed in the depths, You are there. If I rise on the wings of the dawn, if I settle on the far side of the sea, even there Your hand will guide me, Your right hand will hold me fast. If I say, "Surely the darkness will hide me and the light become night around me," even the darkness will not be dark to You; the night will shine like the day, for darkness is as light to You.*

So why do we insist on trying to hide?

Have you ever seen children playing the game Hide and Seek? It's great to watch them! When my step-son Alex was five, we held a little party for him, with three of his cousins. It was great to watch them play together, and it reminded me of the many hours of fun I had playing with my brothers, when I was younger.

As I watched them laughing and having a lot of fun trying to out-hide each other, then helping each other look for the hiders, I saw that there are three types of children playing the game, representative of three types of responses to God.

The first child takes too long to find their hiding place. He runs around from the curtain to under the table, wardrobe to behind the sofa. Then when the seeker shouts out, "Coming ready or not" they become flustered and upset: "No! Wait! I'm not ready! Give me more time!"

This is like the person who tries to fit everything they want to do into their lives, without any thought of the time, or what will happen when time runs out. They run around filling their lives running from this place to that – chasing that dream to that new car, that bigger house to that bigger wage packet, only to find that one day, the Seeker will come back to find His Bride. Their only cry will be "No! Wait! I'm not ready! Give me more time!"

The second type of child is the one who hides and thinks he has the best spot ever, and he will *never* be found. Unbeknown to him, the top of his head can be seen, and when time runs out, the seeker can spot them a mile off, "Caught you!"

This reminds me of those people who try to hide from God. They go to Church, act the part – when other Christians are around, anyway. They can raise their hands in worship or quote the relevant verse at the appropriate time; but away from the Church, away from other believers, they try to hide. There is no difference in this person from the rest of the crowd. Doing what they want, when they want, thinking that if no one sees them then it doesn't matter. But friend, no matter where you think you can hide from God – there is nowhere He will not find you. He knows your heart, not the façade you present to Him. Hide if you will, but the Seeker can spot you a mile off, "Caught you!"

The final child is the one who relishes the moment, as soon as the cry goes out, "Ready or not… here I come!" she giggles excitedly. She can't contain her joy or eagerness and jumps out of her hiding place shouting, "Here I am! Here I am!"

When we *are* ready, we will be like this final child in the game. We will be so excited to hear the final shout of our Yeshua, "Ready or not, here I come!" we will jump up and down with delight shouting, "Here I am! Here I am!"

But this is not a game.

This is real life.

You have an invitation to RSVP; what will it be?

Revelation 19:7: *Let us be glad and rejoice and give Him glory, for the marriage of the Lamb has come, and His wife has made herself ready.*

Dearest reader, the shout is going out…

"Ready or not… He is coming!"

GLOSSARY

Adonai Lord, used in Judaism as a spoken substitute for the ineffable name of God.
Baal Hebrew word for a false god or idol.
Beresheit Genesis – "In the Beginning".
Chuppah A canopy made from material, under which a Jewish marriage is conducted. It literally means to cover or protect.
Elohim The plural form of "El" which is God's Hebrew name first used in Genesis 1:1.
Four cups of the Passover feast:
***The Cup of Sanctification** "I will bring you out from under the burdens of the Egyptians."
***The Cup of Judgment or Deliverance** "I will deliver you from slavery to them."
***The Cup of Redemption** "I will redeem you with an outstretched arm."
***The Cup of Praise or Restoration** "I will take you to be my people, and I will be your God."
Gleaning An agricultural term meaning to gather (grain) which had fallen or been left behind by reapers.
Grafting is a horticultural technique where tissues from one plant are inserted into those of another so the two sets of vascular tissues may join together. Insight into how God's people and new believers in Yeshua were to work together in the Kingdom of God.
Haggadah The Jewish manuscript and traditional order for the Passover Meal; it literally means "telling".
HaMashiach The Messiah
Kiddush A blessing pronounced over the *Kiddush* Cup of wine, which is then passed around the *Shabbat* table before the meal commences.

Kiddushin The betrothal, or sanctification of the man to the woman.

Mikvah The Jewish ritual bath used before people entered the Temple.

Mishkan Literally referring to the Tabernacle, meaning “residence” or “dwelling place”.

Mohar The bride price.

Nisu’in The finalisation of the wedding nuptials.

Selah A Hebrew word meaning to pause and reflect on.

Shabbat Sabbath

Shofar A Jewish trumpet made traditionally from a ram’s horn used in religious ceremonies and as an ancient battle signal.

Shtar Tena’im Document of Conditions presented at the Kiddushin.

Torah The scroll on which the first five books of the Hebrew Scriptures – or the Law – is written, used in synagogue services.

Yeshua HaMashiach Hebrew for Jesus the Messiah.

Yom Kippur The holiest and most solemn religious fast of the Jewish year – the Day of Atonement which follows the Jewish New Year (Rosh Hashanah) focusses on atonement and repentance.

Chapter 1

[1] Please read Genesis Chapter 1.

Chapter 3

[2] This explanation was taken from www.chabad.org which offers detailed explanations of the Jewish betrothal and wedding traditions.
[3] The steps of a traditional Jewish Wedding can be found across the internet, from a variety of sources. I found www.biblestudymanuals.net/jewish_marriage_customs to be useful for the purpose of this study, though I did not spend time looking around the website as a whole, so therefore do not endorse other content of the website.

Chapter 4

[4] The Betrothal blessing is quoted in: http://www.beingjewish.com/cycle/wedding.html
[5] There are many books and teachings which focus on recognising Jesus in the Passover, including Christ in the Passover by Ceil Rosen and Moishe Rosen.
[6] There are many versions of the Haggadah available to buy, should you want to read it for yourself. CMJ has one available to purchase.
[7] This information was taken from http://mikeratliff.wordpress.com/2008/03/26/the-four-cups-of-wine-of-passover/
[8] Communion is also referred to as the Communion Service, Holy Communion, the Lord's Supper or the Eucharist across the denominations.

Chapter 5

[9] The End of the World Cult documentary is still available for viewing on the Channel 4 website: http://www.channel4.com/programmes/the-end-of-the-world-cult; while details of the convictions against Wayne Bent are freely available from Associated Press news-sites, such as: http://www.foxnews.com/story/0,2933,474184,00.html
[10] There are many sources about this news item, but I first read of it on the Daily Mail website on May 3rd 2012: http://www.dailymail.co.uk/news/article-2138660/All-believers-going-destroyed-Religious-sect-spreading-word-ahead-impending-end-world-June-30.html
[11] This quote was taken from: http://www.iamthewitness.com/DarylBradfordSmith_Rothschild.htm
[12] Isaiah 14:12-21 describes in detail the fall of Lucifer who was once an angel of God. When this angel set his heart to try to be

greater than God, God threw him down from heaven, and at the end of time, Jesus will throw satan into the lake of fire (Revelation 20:7-10) along with all those who chose to follow him, rejecting God's invitation through Jesus, whose names are not written in the Book of Life (Revelation 20:15).

Chapter 7

[13] This quote was taken from the website: http://www.wildolive.co.uk/weddings.htm

[14] This is taken from the website: http://www.bibleistrue.com/qna/qna22.htm

Chapter 8

[15] Point number (3) from the definition found on the dictionary.com website.

Chapter 12

[16] A talk was given by Karen Davis (Worship Leader of Kehilat HaCarmel) at the CMJ UK 2011 Conference, of which the author was an organiser, under this same title, "The Warrior Bride" [this is also the sub-title of one of Karen's music CDs]. Although the author was unable to join Karen's seminar, she reflects with joy on the way in which the Holy Spirit plants the same idea in different heads! The Warrior Bride as a thematic title was given to me in 2005 when I originally had a vision to tackle this subject. Karen and I, who are friends, had not shared thoughts on these titles. Obviously the Holy Spirit is at work here! A CD of Karen's seminar is available through CMJ UK.

Chapter 13

[17] Definition provided by Wikipedia – the free online encyclopaedia.

[18] Quote taken from http://en.wikipedia.org/wiki/Vine

[19] Information about the Olive tree taken from Wikipedia search.

[20] Information about the Olive tree taken from Wikipedia search.

[21] Quote taken from http://en.wikipedia.org/wiki/Grafting.

OTHER BOOKS BY GLORY TO GLORY PUBLICATIONS

KINGDOM SEEKERS

What does it mean to seek first the Kingdom of God? Mike Endicott (author of *Heaven's Dynamite*, *Christian Healing*, *Rediscovering Kingdom Healing* and *Pilgrimage*) encourages us to become kingdom seekers. He sets out exciting truths about God's kingdom, showing us something of its attractiveness as well as its centrality to all genuine Christian life and witness. Jesus affirmed that He is the way, the truth and the life, and the author explores some of the powerful implications of that revelation.

THE BIBLE STUDENT

50 exciting studies to help us to explore what the Bible says today!
* does God speak today through the pages of the Bible?
* what is God's message on the key questions that life throws up?
* how consistent is God's revelation in the Old and New Testaments?
An accessible resource for personal and group study, with helpful insights and discussion points for preachers, teachers and all who want to examine key questions in the twenty-first century. Inspired by Joe Church's Every Man a Bible Student, this is a completely revised and updated book, containing new studies and entirely reformatted. Five authors contributed studies: Rev Alex Jacob, Rev David M Moore, Greg Stevenson, Rev Peter Byron-Davies, Peter Sammons.

ONE FLESH

What Jesus teaches about love, relationships and a lot more....
No one enters a relationship for it to go wrong; no one gets married in order to live miserably. There are many happy relationships and many good marriages. Yet there are just as many marriages that go wrong, if the statistics are to be believed. What lessons does the Bible give for finding our life's partner and what happens when we marry. Peter Sammons (author of *The Birth of Christ* and *The Empty Promise of Godism*) tracks through the Old and New Testaments God's progressive revelation of what makes for a lasting and sound relationship. Just what does it take to create a lasting relationship? Suitable for teenage upwards. A useful marriage preparation resource. Suitable for non-Christians.

www.glorytoglory.co.uk